D0896981

PRACTICAL OUTDOOR SURVIVAL

New and Revised

A Modern Approach to Staying Alive in the Wilderness

Len McDougall

THE LYONS PRESS
Guilford, Connecticut
An imprint of The Globe Pequot Press

To Bill Shaw, my mentor and my friend.
You believed in me even when I thought
you were foolish for doing so. Thank you.

To buy books in quantity for corporate use
or incentives, call **(800) 962–0973**
or e-mail **premiums@GlobePequot.com.**

The Lyons Press is an imprint of The Globe Pequot Press.

Text design by Sheryl P. Kober

Library of Congress Cataloging-in-Publication Data is available on file.

ISBN 978-1-59921-171-8

Printed in the United States of America

10 9 8 7 6 5 4 3 2 1

Contents

Contents

Five: **Food**

Six: **Orienteering**

Introduction

In March of 2004 a lone but experienced twenty-nine-year-old woodsman set out across the chest-deep hardpack snow that covered northern Michigan's million-acre Lake Superior State Forest. When he didn't return after three days, his family began to worry (the man was known for turning day outings into spontaneous overnighters). By then his ski tracks had been erased by warming temperatures that melted the compressed snow at better than an inch per day. He has not been seen since. One likely theory is that "rotting" hardpack built up on nothing more than bushes throughout winter suddenly gave way under his weight, sending him crashing down perhaps several feet onto tangled brush and debris. Under such conditions, with nighttime temperatures falling to near zero Fahrenheit, a broken ankle could be fatal.

The first edition of *Practical Outdoor Survival* established itself among outdoors lovers who understand the real difference between hobby survival and actually getting out alive from a perilous situation that could have gone the other way. It's ironic that being equipped to handle a loss of amenities in civilization is commendable (even sanctioned by the U.S. government since 9/11), recreational outdoorsmen who go prepared into a wilderness are often accused of cheating. In a real wilderness survival scenario, there are no rules to break, nothing to prove, and winners of this game may be identifiable as being the ones who are still breathing when it's all over. When losing equals dying, the concept of cheating simply doesn't apply—you can't survive too well.

With that same philosophy, this second edition opens with a chapter on survival equipment, because the naked-into-the-woods theory has always been a myth, and the individual with the most options has always had the best chance of survival. The blessed curse of advancing technology has produced new must-have tools since 1993, but the prerequisites for a survival tool remain unchanged: Every item must be necessary, it has to be as absolutely reliable and rugged as it is feasible, and it needs to perform as many functions as possible. The simplest survival kit fits in a breast pocket, becoming more complex as a prudent outdoorsman outfits for the environment he or she will be visiting, the same as every aboriginal culture has done throughout human history.

As a practical guide to wilderness survival, this book also covers field-proven primitive techniques. Requirements in this category include simplicity and effectiveness. Facing a situation that requires action just to stay alive is tough enough without being complicated, and there is never time or energy to waste on tasks that require extraordinary skill or that might not work. The goal is to obtain a net benefit for every calorie burned, so the primitive survival skills presented here are limited to those that have proved to be the most valuable, efficient, and the easiest to master.

The overall strategy of the new *Practical Outdoor Survival* also remains unchanged: to provide outdoors lovers, from birdwatchers and bikers to kayakers and snowshoers, with an easy answer book to nature's challenges. As opposed to some philosophies, the emphasis here is on being good to oneself. Envision survival as a straight line that extends between life and death: Traveling farther toward the life end results in greater comfort, while moving toward death brings increasing misery. There are many agonies along that line before a victim reaches death. From a purely practical perspective, keeping yourself warm, well fed, rested, and relaxed is plain smart. It isn't usually one big problem that overwhelms victims, but several small troubles that compound, sometimes with a domino effect. It does no good to tough out twenty miles of a thirty-mile hike to safety if you awake the next morning with pneumonia or crippling foot and joint injuries. Becoming dizzy (even fainting) from low blood sugar can be more than hazardous on a rocky trail, while fatigue causes mistakes and erodes your immune system in an environment that does not forgive the sick or weak. Mosquitoes and blackflies won't kill most people, but some of their victims have literally gone mad from their ceaseless torment or became sick from lack of sleep. On the other hand, it's pretty tough to lose hope when you're drowsing next to a warm, bug-free fire after a good dinner, imagining what everyone is going to say when you get back home. Every year roughly a hundred outdoor lovers are found or presumed dead in the United States alone. The purpose of this updated edition of the book that introduced the concept of using every advantage to survive is to help reduce that number to zero.

ONE

The Survival Kit

Be Prepared, the motto of the Boy Scouts of America, is an axiom that should be regarded as a commandment by anyone about to venture into any place where getting help from the civilized world would be difficult to impossible. Five centuries have passed since the Iroquois Nation abandoned bow and arrow and stone tools for iron knives and hatchets and the revolutionary power of the gun. When one's skill at survival was measured day by day, no advantage was unwanted, and the idea of doing things the hard way when it wasn't necessary was almost incomprehensible.

Some tools covered here are recent innovations. Many are updated versions of necessary gear that has been around for centuries, but all have proved their value in the field. How important each item will be depends on the situation at hand, but every survival kit begins with the basic three: knife, fire starter, and compass. From these you can build more advanced kits with more specialized tools for day hiking, snowmobiling, or any backcountry activity. With a little forethought, a few basic survival techniques, and just a pocketful of the right tools, you can have the means to survive whatever nature throws at you. The same progressively larger survival-kit philosophy can be applied to autos and boats, houses, and even commercial buildings. By being ready to address foreseeable problems, the impact of natural disasters could be minimized.

Tools mentioned by name in this chapter have been thoroughly field-tested, some over decades, but they are presented here only as representatives of quality and form, because many will be made obsolete by improved models and innovations. Prices too can vary widely, usually increasing in quality and features offered. An unbending rule is that it has to do the job, whatever its cost.

Survival Knives

It is no exaggeration to say that a knife, in some form, has been critical to human survival since our species learned to manufacture the claws and teeth nature denied us. We require a cutting tool to render food and other elements of an environment into useful forms, even if the tool is simply a sharp-edged slice of rock knocked loose with another stone (that's really all you need to know to fashion a simple stone knife). However, being without a good knife is at least a contradiction of the prime rule of real-world survival: Be prepared.

TYPICAL SURVIVAL KNIFE

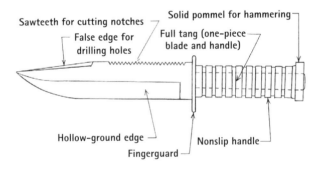

Sawteeth for cutting notches
False edge for drilling holes
Solid pommel for hammering
Full tang (one-piece blade and handle)
Hollow-ground edge
Fingerguard
Nonslip handle

The Blade Trinity

Do not even day hike without at least one good, sharp knife. With a working-class knife, you can cut a rope, whittle a stick, clean a fish, or open a steel can, among a multitude of other tasks that would be difficult to impossible without one. The upside of being forced to create our own tools is that we learned to manufacture cutting, chopping, and digging tools that were superior to anything found in nature, and the finest, strongest blades that ever existed are being made today.

An effective knife philosophy has been dubbed the "blade trinity." It begins with a stout folding knife, preferably with a locking blade and secure pocket-clip carry. Ideally this knife never leaves its owner's person, even when the owner is sleeping. The blade needs to be at least three inches long to be field functional, preferably made from strong, hard stainless steel by a manufacturer that has a reputation to protect. Beyond that, it needs to feel comfortable to its user, because a knife that feels clumsy is dangerous.

For full-day and longer outings, a dedicated fixed-blade belt knife is called for. This is the workhorse blade, capable of prying apart stumps and ripping through dead logs in search of edible insects or fish bait, chopping and whittling a bow stave, or hacking through the pelvic bone of a deer. Built more heavily than a conventional hunting knife, it needs to have a blade at least five inches long to give it leverage as a pry bar, a strong but sharp tip that can punch through hide and bone, and a weatherproof blade of stainless or epoxy-coated alloy (or the newer indestructible beta titanium). It needs a secure finger guard and nonslip hilt to keep a user's hand from sliding onto the blade, and its pommel should be made for use as a hammer. Its sheath must be absolutely secure around the knife and on the belt—Lose your knife, lose your life—and it needs to incorporate a large cargo pocket for the small compass and fire-starting tools that make the knife a survival kit.

For fully equipped outings, like backpacking, snowmobiling, or kayaking, there is no reason to deny oneself the tremendous survival advantage provided by a heavy machete or "camp knife."

These rugged tools typically have ten inches of blade, built intentionally heavy to maximize chopping and prying power, but shorter than a jungle machete to permit swinging it in thick brush. The handles are ergonomically contoured, and molded from shock-absorbing, unbreakable rubber, and most incorporate a finger guard and a hooked pommel to help keep the knife from slipping out of tired hands.

For day hikes, Columbia River's M21-04 pocket-clip folder is a good choice.
If terrain and common sense dictate having more insurance, Schrade's Extreme
is a survival toolbox. For full-blown survival outfits, adding Ontario Knife's
powerful SP-8 machete gives a survivalist the ability to transform his surroundings
into home.

Field-Proven Folding Knives

Benchmade Rukus $260.00
Blade-Tech Rijbak $265.00
Columbia River M21 $70.00

Field-Proven Survival Knives

Mission Knives titanium-blade MPK10-Ti $426.00
Ontario Knife RAT-7 $70.00
Schrade Extreme $50.00
Ka-Bar Black Camp Knife $60.00

Field-Proven Machetes
Ontario Knife SP-8 $70.00
Ka-Bar Cutlass Machete
$80.00

Survival Compasses

Every survival kit incorporates a simple magnetic compass, because every outdoorsman needs one—that point cannot be overstressed. Humans do not possess the magnetic sense of direction common to most animals, and anthropologists believe that we probably never had the sensory connections to "feel" the pull of earth's magnetic North Pole. There are numerous natural methods of discerning direction (see chapter 6), but no navigational tool is more reliable than the same

Today's survival knife is a system. Shown: Mission Knives' indestructible Katrina SAR knife with Beta titanium blade and cargo sheath equipped with map flashlight and Strike Force flint-and-steel.

magnetic compass that has been guiding sailors across vast seas since the time of the pharaohs.

The only thing any conventional magnetic compass actually does is to point at the earth's magnetic north pole when held parallel to the earth so that its indicator moves freely. It does that all the time, regardless of weather and without batteries or satellites. The most valuable function of knowing the direction of north is that it provides a steady reference point, which means that a hiker can always travel in a straight line in any direction he or she chooses, and that alone is enough to get out of the woods in most cases.

Pocket Compass

A must-have for any backwoods activity, this most vital orienteering tool is also the smallest and least expensive, offering the added advantage of carrying a backup, should one be lost or broken. Especially suited for short-distance navigation, a pocket compass all but guarantees that you are never lost. It should be liquid filled to give it a smooth, bounce-free movement, be encased in a sturdy plastic capsule, and have a lanyard hole that enables it to be worn around the neck. Avoid pin-on compasses that are notorious for being lost when you need them; a pocket compass should never leave its owner's person.

Map Compass

For longer-distance multiday backpack trips, the next step up in utility is a map compass whose clear base permits laying the instrument directly on top of a map. By aligning both compass and map to north, an orienteer can in effect get an aerial view of the surrounding terrain. The dial (bezel) of the compass can be employed as a protractor for triangulating, while the base edges are marked with distance scales (rulers) to accommodate various map scales. Most of these compasses also incorporate a magnifying glass for reading small print.

Sighting Compasses

Sighting compasses can do what a map compass can do, but they also carry a set of onboard sights—much like a gun—that permit the instrument to precisely target any identifiable landmark (mountain peak, the tip of a peninsula, etc.). This allows you to read the number of degrees between magnetic north and the landmark, relative to your own position. With an accurate bearing from two or more identifiable geographic points, and some simple addition or subtraction, you can transfer that information to a map to determine where you are with considerable accuracy. Most sighting compasses are either *prismatic*, with a folding sighting mirror, or *lensatic*, with a magnifying lens for reading bezel numbers, but both types can provide an accurate bearing, or azimuth, to any visible landmark.

Field-Proven Compasses

Brunton 11HNL, with
whistle $12
Silva Trekker Type 20
$20
Brunton SightMaster
$80
Brunton 8099 Eclipse
$90

Brunton 8099 Pro Eclipse compass

Maps

A map is an aerial view of a geographic section of land. By using your compass to orient map north to magnetic north, all terrain features shown on the map are where they appear to be, relative to your own position. The lake it shows on the right (east) is indeed east of your location; that road shown north (straight ahead) of your location can be reached by heading north. Having a preview of the surrounding area, and trails that run through it, permits plotting an efficient course while avoiding unpleasant terrain. A map also shows landmarks that can be expected to lie ahead, as well as a scale of distances.

In a pinch, even a gas station map is better than none, but more detailed trail maps are available from state conservation department field offices. In mountain country, where it helps to know terrain elevations, very good topographical maps are available from the U.S. Geographical Survey (see www.usgs.gov).

Fire-Starting Tools

Wilderness survival classes cannot be canceled on account of weather, and the young professionals who had booked a week in

Lake Superior State Forest with me during November were learning that backcountry survival training can become actual experience in a hurry. Daytime temps never rose above forty, it was freezing at night, and the frigid, wind-driven rain never stopped. It was impossible to keep dry, but water-repellent synthetic clothing kept our bodies performing comfortably in the kind of weather that terrified outdoorsmen of even a generation ago.

When night fell and air temperature dropped twenty degrees, a hot supper and warm fire were crucial for replenishing core body heat. That meant having an absolute ability to make a fire, regardless of conditions.

A buckskin-clad traditionalist with a bow and drill cannot start a fire under the conditions just described, and veteran survival instructors know that. They also know that no skill is more likely to save your life anywhere on earth than the ability to make fire. With fire, you can survive bitter cold, fend off bugs and animals, signal for help, and ensure that everything you eat or drink is free of pathogens; without fire, doing any one of those things might be impossible.

For fifteen years, the main tool in my fire-making outfit has been the Strike Force flint and steel. Its half-inch flint rod throws sparks like an arc welder, and it has never failed to ignite natural tinder in any weather. If it did fail, a tinder cube in the handle lights easily and burns hotly in the wettest conditions. If I'm backpacking or kayak camping, I keep one of these tools in a cargo pocket of my trousers all the time, with a spare stashed in a day pack or backpack.

Disposable butane lighters have been a cheap, dependable source of fire for three decades, although they weren't available to generations before now. I have one of these at all times, and because of their insignificant weight and price, I have several scattered throughout my gear. When its butane supply is depleted, the lighter can continue to make fire if you remove the metal hood and strike its weak spark against finely frayed tissue paper, cotton batting, or cotton char cloth. A Zippo liquid-fuel lighter has been a permanent resident of my right hip pocket since I was a boy. It has proved valuable enough to merit carrying a small bottle of fuel and spare flints in my most basic day-hiking pack. Priced at around $15 for unadorned models, Zippo lighters have been a mainstay of backwoods fire-making outfits for nearly a century.

In 2007 Zippo introduced its Outdoor Utility Lighter (OUL), a butane-fired hand torch that survived rugged field trials to become a valued emergency fire starter. Priced at about $35, the OUL produces a strong wind-resistant flame from a stout chromed barrel that easily lights jarred candles and lantern wicks. Submersion in water can take the lighter out of action until its innards dry, so backpackers should keep it ziplocked in a plastic bag, but the OUL has not yet failed to make fire for me.

Matches have had a place in survival kits for two centuries, from waterproof "lifeboat" types with varnished oversize heads to paper matchbooks that are still offered free to customers at many businesses. Lifeboat matches can be pricey, at about 15 cents per match. Paper matches sealed in a ziplock bag can be carried for years until needed, and they are cheap enough to scatter thousands throughout backpacks, vehicles, and home. Wooden kitchen matches are even better, but be sure to include the box's striker strip when you repackage them in a watertight container.

For a guaranteed flame, you need a tinder that will light easily and burn hotly under any conditions. Most environments provide ample tinders, like dry grass, birch bark, reindeer moss, and pine pitch, but having a weatherproof tinder in your pocket at all times can be reassuring.

Manufactured tinder sticks, ribbons, and pastes can be found in sporting goods stores, and there are home-brewed tinders— like cotton balls saturated with petroleum jelly—but my longtime favorite is the fire wick. Made by saturating cotton laundry string (or wool felt) with molten paraffin (canning wax), then cutting the cooled and hardened sections to a desired length, fire wicks cannot get too wet to burn, they light easily by fraying one end, and they have an indefinite shelf life. You have to make them yourself, but

The Strike Force flint-and-steel (left) is the author's favorite never-fail fire starter, but in terms of bang for your buck, a disposable butane lighter can't be beat; wax-saturated cotton-string "fire wicks" are contained in a screw-top pill bottle, and one is burning atop the snow.

they cost roughly one dollar per two hundred wicks, which makes it economical to spread fire wicks throughout your gear.

Under actual survival conditions, the need for fire will always be greatest under conditions that are prohibitive to getting one started, so people who venture off the beaten path for even a day hike should be a little obsessive about their ability to make fire. When the consequences of not having one can include miseries like biting bugs, pneumonia, parasitic and bacterial infections, and lying injured until someone stumbles upon you, there is no such thing as cheating: There are only those who come back from a wilderness safe and sound, and those who did something else.

Bow and Drill

I do not teach the bow and drill fire starter during three-day basic survival courses. It is a difficult tool to master, especially if you have to construct it on the spot, and with so many cheap pocket-size fire starters available it's not hard to have at least one of them at all times. That being said, it's reassuring to know that you could start a fire with a bow and drill if you had to, so by all means practice this technique. Just don't bet your life on it; there are situations where it won't work, and those are generally the times when you really need a fire.

The concept of the bow and drill is simple: a wooden drill, or spindle, made from dried softwood such as poplar, pine, or basswood, is spun back and forth rapidly against a "fire board" made from any slab of dried wood that will produce enough friction and heat to cause the tinder to smolder. With a bit of practice the entire tool can be constructed in about thirty minutes, and a fire started in another twenty minutes. This doesn't compare to the instant fire produced by modern fire-starting aids.

Construction of the bow and drill is also simple. The tool has five basic parts: the bow, bowstring, handle, fire board, and drill. The drill is made from a straight, dry, barkless piece of softwood, usually a dead sapling. The ideal drill should be dead and dry, about eight inches long, at least one inch in diameter, and as round and straight as possible to minimize wobbling during rotation. The drill may be shaved and shaped with a knife. Once a suitable drill has been chosen, the bottom section is whittled to a dull point and the top is rounded as smoothly as possible. Use coarse rock or sandstone to smooth imperfections from the finished drill.

The drill's top spins inside a palm-size handle made from a piece of dried wood about three inches wide, six inches long, and two inches thick. If possible, the handle should be made from a hardwood like oak, cherry, or maple. The edges should be smoothed to fit comfortably in your palm. Using the point of your knife as a drill, dig out and shape a rounded hole that matches the top rounded portion of the drill. To make the two pieces fit together more closely, rotate the drill by hand in the hole of the handle. The addition of a little sand will help to smooth the rough surfaces in the hole. If possible, the finished handle detent should be lubricated with wax or grease to decrease friction between the drill top and the handle.

The fire board is made from a piece of coarse-grained wood about six inches wide, twelve to eighteen inches long, and one inch thick, and as flat as possible on both sides. It's usually best to make the board by splitting slabs from a section of dead (but not rotten) poplar or pine log with a strong, sharp knife or hatchet until an acceptable board is obtained. Once a board has been selected, drill a hole into one corner using the tip of the knife. The hole should be conical, about one-half inch deep and one-half inch wide at the top. The exact location of the hole on the board isn't important, but it should be about one-eighth inch from the edge of the board at its widest point.

When the hole is finished, a downward-sloping notch is cut into the one-eighth inch remaining between its edge and the outside of the board, about one-half inch deep and just slightly narrower than the drill hole. This notch provides a chute to direct hot, powdered wood, or "char," onto the tinder.

The bow is made from a green branch of willow, cedar, or any other springy wood. It may also be made from a young sapling. The bow should ideally be about one inch in diameter by two feet in length. Notch both ends with a shallow groove to help hold the bowstring in place. If the bow you've selected has a natural curve, use it to your advantage.

The bowstring can be made from nearly any type of sturdy cord, such as a shoelace or a length of parachute cord. Tie one end to the bow using a slipknot, making sure the cord fits securely into the notch at that end. Pull the string until it's taut, but not so tight that it flexes the bow, and tie the free end to the opposite end of the bow, again making certain that it nestles snugly into the notch.

With the bow and drill now assembled, hold the bow horizontal to the ground in your right hand (opposite if you're a lefty) and place the drill, rounded end up, between the bow and the string.

Wrap the string around the drill one time and place the pointed end of the drill into the hole in the fire board.

Place the handle on top of the drill with your left hand, making sure that the rounded top of the drill fits loosely but securely into the hole in the handle. Kneel with your right knee resting on the ground

USING THE BOW AND DRILL

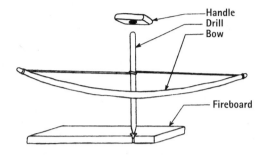

and your left foot on the fire board to help hold it in place. Rest your left elbow on the left knee and press downward firmly but not hard on the handle. With the bow still held horizontal to the ground, begin moving it back and forth with a smooth sawing motion. The drill will spin, first in one direction, then the other, with each stroke. If the drill doesn't spin freely, ease up a bit on the handle.

As the drill spins against the fire board it will begin to heat up from friction. A sprinkling of sand in the fire board hole will help to increase the friction. As you continue to saw the bow back and forth, the drill tip will begin to smoke, and a charred brown powder will begin to accumulate in the fire board notch. As this powder begins to fill the notch and fall upon the pile of dried tinder (crushed dry grass, cotton fibers, powdered reindeer moss) placed before and under the notch opening, it will begin to glow. At this point your arm will feel tired enough to fall off, but don't quit yet. When enough of this heated wood powder, sometimes called *char*, falls upon the tinder, it too will begin to smoke.

As soon as the tinder is smoking freely, immediately drop the bow and drill and gather the tinder in your cupped palms. Very gently blow into the pile; a prolonged, gentle blow is best. When the tinder catches fire, lay the flaming mass gently onto a small platform of sticks placed side by side on the ground, and add more dry tinder to increase the intensity of the heat.

The next step is to pile very small dry twigs (less than a pencil in diameter to start with) in a tepee arrangement on top of the burning tinder, taking care not to add weight that can compress the tinder and inhibit burning. As these small twigs begin to flame, add more small twigs until a bed of coals below makes the fire self-sustaining. Finally, add progressively larger twigs and branches until the fire is large enough for warmth or cooking.

Fishing Gear

A basic angling outfit is downright cheap—fifty hooks, a hundred-yard spool of monofilament line, and a dozen or so split shot sinkers go for under five bucks at department stores. An assortment of long-shank hooks works best for catching a variety of fish—and for removing hooks after the catch. Hooks can be carried in their original containers, stuck into the perimeter of a cork, or laid onto a strip of electrical tape, then covered with another strip of tape to form a bandolier of sorts.

Your split shot sinkers should be in a variety of weights to accommodate current and wave forces; figure a minimum of two weights per set. These can be carried conveniently stuck between two opposing strips of tape, pinched onto a length of line, or in a watertight pill bottle—anything that will keep them together in a pocket.

Fishing line may be monofilament, or the newer braided-fiber lines, but it should be rated to work at ten pounds (or more). A one-hundred-yard spool fits into any fanny pack, and can also serve as snare line or for heavy-duty sewing jobs. Alternatively, several yards can be wound and taped in place around a pill bottle that also holds sinkers and hooks, maybe even Swedish Pimples or other "jigging" lures, and can itself serve as a fishing float or bait container.

Field-Expedient Fishing Gear

You can't fit an entire tackle box into a breast pocket; some useful items, like fishing floats or "bobbers," are just too bulky. Fortu-

MAKESHIFT FISHING GEAR

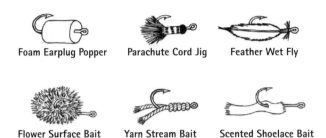

Foam Earplug Popper   Parachute Cord Jig   Feather Wet Fly

Flower Surface Bait   Yarn Stream Bait   Scented Shoelace Bait

nately many of the items a survival angler needs to enhance the chances of landing dinner are easily made from materials at hand.

Fishing Floats

Day-feeding panfish are usually good candidates for a baited hook that is held off the bottom by a float attached overhead. When a fish grabs for the bait, the activity is transferred to the float, causing it to jerk with each tug on the hook. When the bobber is pulled underwater, or begins to travel across the surface, a tug against the line is usually all it takes to set the hook.

Making a bobber is as simple as finding a dry twig that floats. Typical candidates are about six inches long, an inch in diameter, and contrast well against the water's surface—scraping away the surface of weather-darkened wood makes the float lighter in color. With a gentle, controlled rocking motion, drive the edge of your folding knife crosswise into one end of the float to split it about two inches into its length. Gently work your fishing line into that split, where it will be held in place by friction. Adjust the float depth by sliding it up or down on the line, and toss it into the water. If available, a good float can also be made in the same way from the grub-created ball, known as a gall, that often forms on the stem of tall goldenrod, which is found growing near water throughout the United States.

Artificial Baits

Normally associated with rod-and-reel casting outfits, artificial baits can catch fish for primitive anglers too. Manufactured lures, from floating flies to small spinners and pimples that can be pulled back and forth or jigged through the water, can usually be fitted into a pill-bottle fishing kit.

Effective fishing lures can also be made on the spot. One field-expedient "popper" floating lure that has taken enough surface-feeding fish to become a permanent part of my tackle box is simply a foam-rubber earplug slid onto a long-shank hook. Wet flies can be made by threading an inch of shoelace or parachute cord onto a hook, fraying the hook end of the cord to make it wave in the water, then melting the eye end into a heavy blob that causes the jigged lure to behave like a pimple. Many a trout have been caught on nothing more than a couple of inches of brightly colored yarn tied to a hook.

Also effective is taking a section of a bird's feather and tying it to a hook shank with a couple dozen turns of thread. This original fishing fly may be floated or weighted, jigged, or just twitched occasionally. Alternatively, tufts of fur, particularly the coarser hairs of deer, can be wound into place on the hook to form "whiskers" that may enhance the fly's attractiveness. To make a wavy-tail wet fly, you can even use a lock of your own hair.

Shelter

In no culture have humans failed to build houses. From the carved sandstone cliff houses of the Pueblos to the thatched huts of Indochina to the Eskimo igloo, humans in every environment require shelter from the elements. For whatever reason, nature has seen fit to deny us natural protection from inclement weather, and we are the only earthlings who can die of exposure at any latitude. Any ambient temperature of less than 98.6 Fahrenheit is stealing heat from our bodies, and our naked skin must be insulated to retain warmth or even the strongest human will eventually succumb to cooling of the internal organs. To put that in perspective, a victim whose core temperature is lowered by three degrees curls into an involuntary fetal position to minimize heat loss from internal organs. Lower the core temperature by five degrees, and the person will die unless immediately hospitalized, and sometimes that is too late. Throw in a cooling rain and the deceptively chilling effect of wind, and an unprotected person could literally die of exposure anywhere on earth. And if a cold night doesn't kill one outright, nothing hammers the immune system like hypothermia.

Bivy Shelters

The first edition of this book was written during a twelve-year period when I didn't consider any tent worthy of lugging around on my back. Instead, I carried a compactly rolled ten-foot-by-ten-foot square of plastic sheeting (Varathane), which I sometimes hung over convenient tree limbs as a roof to crawl under with my backpack, or draped across a shelter frame to provide all-around protection. I sometimes had to sleep wearing a mosquito head net, but a wool blanket protected my body, and the plastic itself could be pulled together to keep most mosquitoes outside. At least it didn't leak, holes were easily patched with a strip of duct tape, and it blocked the wind entirely. A sheet of Varathane or, later on, a lightweight tarp, was basically all the shelter one needed to survive inclement weather.

Today compact one- or two-person "bivy" shelters stuff into a sack the size of a loaf of bread, with about the same weight and requiring only slightly more setup time than just crawling under a tarp. Probably not for the claustrophobic, bivies are designed to offer fast and complete protection from wind, rain, and all biting bugs. Prices for good ones currently begin at about $100.

More basic, and cheaper, are the plastic or tarpaulin shelters mentioned above. For short hikes, you might opt to tuck an aluminum-laminated Mylar "space blanket" into a breast pocket. While it's no replacement for even a good wool blanket when it comes to keeping you warm, the space blanket does block wind and rain and reflects at least some body heat. Or the blanket can be

In some weather, shelter might be the most critical survival need, and today's ultralight "bivouac," or bivy, shelters give even day hikers survival capabilities that weren't available to their fathers.

fastened overhead to form an eighty-four-inch-by-fifty-four-inch mirrored roof that is visible for miles from the air.

Weighing two ounces and retailing for about $3 at most sporting goods stores, the space blanket is worth carrying.

Cordage

A common neurosis among veteran woodsmen is their reluctance to cut the cord or rope they carry. This apparent phobia is actually a statement of how much experience has taught them to appreciate the value of a good rope. Nothing in nature equals the strength and durability of man-made cordage, whether hanging a deer for skinning, lashing together a snowshoe frame, repairing a broken backpack strap, or just replacing a broken shoelace. Two hundred feet of nylon packaging string, with a thirty-pound working load, retails for about $3, and several yards can be carried coiled and forgotten in a hip pocket.

SURVIVAL KNOTS

Square knot: Fastens two ends together

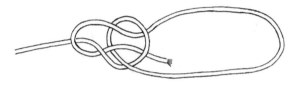

Bowline: Non-tightening loop

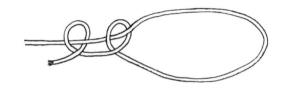

Double half-hitch: Slipknot for loops that tighten when pulled

Three of the most important knots a survivalist needs to commit to memory.

The king of survival cordage is the 550-pound-test parachute cord sold by army surplus retailers for about 10 cents per foot. Be aware that there is also what's called a "mil-spec" version of para cord that looks similar, except that it has thin fibers inside its jacket, not the smaller cords of authentic parachute cord, and is rated for about half the work load.

Beyond that, the cordage someone has on hand in a survival situation should match the activity.

Jacket or thigh pockets should carry at least an extra boot lace; day packs or fanny packs can easily carry fifty or more feet of para cord, a spool of nylon string, or both; and the list goes on, up to tow ropes in four-wheel-drives. The uses for cordage are endless, and there is no good reason not to have as functional a supply on hand as your activity permits.

Flashlights

Prior to the twentieth century, human activities virtually stopped when the sun set. Most workdays ended, travel was limited, and even wars were postponed until dawn. But it wasn't superstition that kept the Blackfeet from attacking at night and farmers bolted in their cabins with a gun that was "loaded for bear"; it was simple fear spawned by the realization that our species is all but blind at night. Stealth was not possible when one couldn't see what one was tripping over, but ankle and knee injuries were possible, and it has always scared strong men to realize that they alone are blind in a night forest while all large predators have excellent night vision. It was better to just build a fire and stay put until you could see again.

Today flashlights have become dependable enough to be an integral part of every survival kit, and there is no reason to be blind at night. For two decades, my belt has carried a Mini Maglite AA flashlight—today with low-drain LED light and rechargeable batteries (about $15)—and I have a AAA Maglite Solitaire on my key ring (about $5) and another on a lanyard inside my survival knife's cargo pouch. Being able to see on the darkest night makes life easier in general and opens new horizons in night navigation.

Signals

A person stuck in a wilderness-survival dilemma generally has two choices: try to make one's own way back to civilization as efficiently and intelligently as possible, or stay put and hope that someone else will come to the rescue. Which one is best depends on the situation, on the person's fitness to travel, and the tools at hand. The uninjured survivor of a "soft" plane crash in the Canadian Rockies in late summer might be smart to hike through the passes shown on the map before they are choked by deep snow. The same survivor would be foolish to try that in late autumn, when the chance of being caught in the middle of one of those blizzards would be high.

If a situation demands staying put, you will probably welcome help from outside, especially if medical problems are part of the equation. In light of the overwhelming job faced by search-and-rescue (SAR) personnel—and the budget constraints of these often poorly funded agencies—it behooves anyone who envisions the possibility of needing rescue to be well equipped to get that help message across effectively.

Flares

Signal flares are a tried-and-true method of attracting attention but only if those who might notice it are within sight. Probably most recognizable are the classic orange break-action single-shot pistols commonly seen in plane crash movies. Available in 25 mm or 12-gauge caliber, usually with an attached bandolier of four extra cartridges, these plastic guns can launch a sixteen-thousand candlepower "meteor" flare to about four hundred feet, with a burn time of about seven seconds.

Several other types and sizes of aerial flares are available, usually with cylinder-shape tube launchers, some reusable, and in a variety of colors. Marine flares include parachute types that can stay aloft for more than half a minute, and even flares that are designed to burn out before landing to minimize the danger of a forest fire. Nonlaunched road-type flares can be useful for sending a bright signal from high or otherwise open ground, but they have probably proved most valuable for starting fires.

Many outdoorsmen do not carry flares, and in spite of its life-saving potential, an aerial flare is not always useful. Mountain climbers should not make an ascent without pencil flares; no bush or island-hopper plane is airworthy without an extensive survival kit that includes pistol and flares; every canoe or kayak should have some type of aerial flares on board. Conversely, a canoeist or especially a backpacker under the thick canopy of an Ontario forest might be better off trading the weight and bulk of a flare kit for something that will prove more useful in a close environment.

Signal of Threes

Anyone in need of rescue needs to know the signal of threes, because it is simple, and likely to be recognized by SAR personnel. For hunters, three rifle shots into the air has been a call for help since repeating arms were invented, but the same principle applies to almost anything that can be used to create an abrupt sight or sound: two stones clacked together from the side of a mountain, three flashes from a bright flashlight or headlights, three loud whistles or blasts from a horn, or three hard whacks of a stout pole against a tree trunk (this may bring Bigfoot researchers).

Sending a signal of threes means having someone close enough to see or hear it, so try to match signal to terrain. Flashes from the brightest torch are difficult for a pilot to see through a heavy forest canopy, and a signal mirror might not work at all—both of these need to be sent from high, open places that are visible from many miles. Audible signals can be more versatile because they cannot be blocked from sight, but they too should be generated from open country—if sound echoes there, it's a good spot.

More noticeable, if not recognizable, are the Morse code letters SOS—an antiquated abbreviation for Save Our Ship that has become synonymous with any plea for help. The letter *S* is represented by three dots (• • •), which translates into three short signals. The letter *O* is three dashes (– – –), or three long signals. To send an SOS with a flashlight, for example, the person signaling would flash the beam with three short bursts (*S*), followed by three bursts of longer duration (*O*), and finally three more short bursts (*S*). The SOS signal can also be made with sounds, as with a whistle. Knocking rocks together or "tree clubbing" creates sounds (signals) that are uncontrollably brief. In these cases, the dashes and dots are represented by the pauses between the sounds, and not the sounds themselves.

Signal Mirrors

In open country where you can get a clear shot at directing a beam of reflected sunlight onto a distant target where someone might notice the flash, a signal mirror can be a life saver. The best of these are the molded Lexan with a star-shaped sighting hole and the ability to float on water (about $12 in sporting goods stores). While facing the sun, look with one eye through the mirror's sighting hole, then place the target in the center of the sighting hole (this may be difficult if the target is a moving airplane). Tip the mirror one way then the other, keeping your target fixed in the sighting hole, until a bright spot appears in its center. Place that bright spot onto the target, and reflected sunlight will be directed onto that spot. Move the spot on and off the target to send flash signals.

Ground-to-Air Signals

The ability to signal overflying aircraft may be vital. The simplest method is to keep a fire burning brightly through the night, then keep the hot coals producing smoke during daylight hours by fueling them with wet, half-rotted wood. Because of the threat of forest fires pilots are always on the alert for smoke and flames.

Other ground-to-air signals include stamping out the letters SOS in snow or on an open beach, or forming the letters with logs in a clearing. Better are the internationally recognized emergency ground-to-air signals shown in the illustration on p. 24, formed the same ways, but with a more extensive vocabulary to transmit specific, urgent needs, such as medical assistance.

Emergency ground-to-air signals can be made with pieces of wood or in the snow or sand.

INTERNATIONAL EMERGENCY
GROUND-TO-AIR SIGNALS

Which Way?	This Way	OK to Land	I'm OK
No	Yes	I Don't Understand	I Need a Compass
I'm Hurt	I Need Medical Assistance	I Can't Proceed	I Need Food and Water

Personal Locator Beacons (PLBs)

PLBs are battery-operated one-way transmitters that send signals at frequencies that are monitored by SAR receivers. A fallen mountain climber who trips his or her PLB sends a unique distress signal to an overhead satellite, which relays the signal to a mission control on earth. Each PLB transmits a digital identification that is registered to its owner, and GPS-equipped PLB models bring rescuers within feet of the beacon. This enables SAR paramedics to arrive on scene, without having to search for the victim, and armed with insulin or other drugs the victim may need but does not

USING A SIGNAL MIRROR
(drawing courtesy of Survival, Inc)

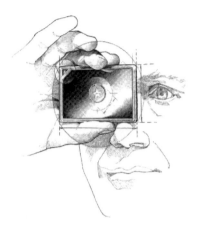

have. PLBs are registered to the National Oceanic and Atmospheric Administration (www.beaconregistration.NOAA.gov) at no charge, but bear in mind that some states pass along the very significant cost of a rescue in an invoice to the rescued party. Unit prices begin at around $300 for basic 406 MHz models, about $500 if you want one equipped with GPS. Designed to be worn around the neck, the units are waterproof, usually to three meters, with a battery life of up to forty hours.

One drawback is that the signal, as with satellite telephones, can be affected or even blocked by terrain and overhead canopy, so units should be triggered from open terrain (preferably where a helicopter can land).

Survival Firearms
Half a millennium has passed since an Iroquois chief complained that in a single generation the hunters of his tribe had forgotten how to take game with a bow and arrow. When it comes to putting fresh meat on the fire, no hunting weapon has ever had the

accuracy and killing power of a rifle, and today's guns and ammo are better than ever.

Whether you need a gun will be determined by local laws and your own judgment.

Better to have it and not need it than need it and not have it is a guideline of survival, but there are only a few regions where having a rifle strapped to your backpack won't generate suspicion.

Basically, the value of having a gun increases the farther one gets from civilization. Much disagreement exists about which gun and caliber is the best for survival, but viable choices narrow quickly when you begin to consider the needs your gun will likely have to meet. Foremost is the fact that no firearm is more than a club without ammunition, so cartridges need to be small but powerful enough to kill game. The gun itself needs to be lightweight and convenient to carry—many a trophy has been missed because a hunter left his gun leaning against a tree.

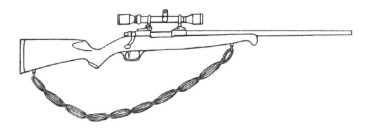

Survival Rifle

The Ultimate Survival Rifle

After much experimentation, my brass tacks survival gun these past three decades has been a light, fast-handling rifle chambered in .22 long rifle caliber. A standard "brick" of .22 long rifle ammo weighs four pounds and contains five-hundred rounds, individually packaged in boxes of fifty rounds each. Sealed in ziplock bags with moisture-absorbing silica packets, the entire brick can be carried in a jacket pocket or spread throughout your gear, and cartridges carried this way remain functional for more than ten years.

The potential power of a .22 long rifle bullet tends to be dangerously underestimated. At the muzzle, a plain old Winchester T22 cartridge with forty-grain lead bullets has a velocity of 1,150 feet per second (fps) and 117 foot pounds of force. At one hundred yards, the bullet retains a velocity of 976 fps and a respectable 85 foot pounds of energy. Loadings in the 1,150 fps category have proved most accurate for sighting in and plinking, and they are the least expensive—currently about $1.50 per box of fifty—but lack the shocking power to reliably take game larger than a squirrel. They will, however, consistently punch through four inches of pine at fifty yards.

When the target is live food, switch the ammo in your pockets to one of the hypervelocity long rifle cartridges that were introduced in the 1970s. Souped up to muzzle velocities beyond 1,400 fps, these cartridges offer premium killing power for about $2.50 per box of fifty. Proven performers include Remington's Yellowjacket (thirty-six-grain truncated hollow point, 1,410 fps, 159 foot pounds), CCI's Quik-Shok (thirty-two-grain fragmenting hollow point, 1,640 fps, 191 foot pounds). For game animals under ten pounds, you might opt for the less explosive power of CCI's expanding Small Game Bullet (SGB forty-grain flat nose, 1,235 fps, 135 foot pounds).

In terms of accuracy, no caliber beats the .22 long rifle to fifty yards, and all brands are dangerously powerful at more than twice that range. Benchrest tests using five types of ammunition, two rifles (an auto and a bolt), and two shooters revealed that accuracy decreased slightly as velocity increased, but every loading could be counted on to hold five shots within two inches at fifty yards. Beyond fifty yards, all bullets were very susceptible to wind drift. It was helpful to note that points of impact between all brands varied only a few tenths of an inch at fifty yards, meaning that you can sight in with target ammunition, then switch to more lethal hunting cartridges without rezeroing your sights. If a squirrel peeks at you from around a tree at forty yards, you have every reason to expect that your .22 can hit it in the eye.

Like their ammo, guns that shoot .22 long rifle ammunition tend to be lightweight and inexpensive. Virtually any make or model can suffice as a survival rimfire (first guns should not be semiautomatic), but most need a paint job that will endure exposure to the elements. This is as simple as suspending the barreled action by a cord, then spraying it with several coats of black primer. Take care not to over-spray inside the (taped-off) trigger or action, and allow each coat to dry thoroughly before applying the next. I like to harden the dried primer with a brushed-on layer of clear acrylic (floor wax). If the fin-ish gets scraped in the woods, just spot spray that area again when you get home. In the quarter century since a handful of people started using it, this protective coating has been applied to many firearms that are exposed to the elements for days, even months, at a time.

The primary sight on any survival rifle should be telescopic (I like to keep iron sights as backup). Today's scopes are more rugged and watertight than ever, even the inexpensive ones, and a $40 model will suffice, providing it has at least a one-inch tube, 32 mm objective lens, and magnification of 4x to a maximum of 10x. Features of a good scope include a sealed, nitrogen-filled body, JIS Class 6 waterproofing, and light-gathering metallic lens coatings (preferably phase coated and applied to both sides).

Grooved ring mounts that make the gun and scope perform as a unit must be well fitted and tight; I recommend sticking with name brands like Uncle Mike's. On my own working guns, the fitted scope mounts are permanently affixed to the receiver by a seam of epoxy, which strengthens the mount and makes changing scopes easier.

My preferred sling is the Ranger sling. This easily made, extremely functional long-arm sling consists of about fifty feet of nylon cord or rope looped back and forth through the swivels at a length that best suits its user. The final ten feet is wound spiral fashion around the loops to bind them together and tied off at the nearest swivel. The completed sling is quiet and comfortable, easy to get into, and serves as a ready supply of strong cordage.

Half the fun of having an ultimate survival rifle lies in its creation, and some become personal reflections of their owner, like the often one-of-a-kind muzzleloaders carried by mountain people of old. Nearly every .22 rifle made today is capable of remarkable accuracy and killing power; give it an immunity to weather, a reliable sight, hypervelocity expanding-bullet ammo, and a few practical add-ons, and you can transform almost any plinking .22 into a deadly serious survival firearm for under $250.

Field-Proven Survival Rifles (.22 long rifle caliber only)
Marlin Model 925 bolt action $200.00
Savage Arms Mark II-F bolt-action $180.00
Marlin Model 60 semiauto $200.00

Marksmanship
In both World Wars, soldiers who faced American troops in battle were mortified to learn that the uncultured farm boys they shot it out with were often highly skilled sharpshooters and armed with better rifles than most of them had ever seen. For these citizen-soldiers, hunting and fishing had not been sports but were integral parts of living in the still vast American wilderness where a missed shot could mean a missed meal.

Easy to learn but difficult to master, rifle marksmanship is a procedure consisting of several smaller processes working together. First is proper sight alignment: Place the rifle butt against your preferred shoulder with the stock securely nestled into the hollow of the shoulder between the breast and upper arm. Lean forward slightly, never backward, and rest the stock under the barrel in your opposite hand, as close to the gun's balance point as you can determine (usually at the lug screw that connects stock and hardware).

If the gun is equipped with telescopic sights, adjust your cheekbone on the upper ridge of the stock until the sight picture in the scope is as bright and clear as it can be. The proper eye relief, the distance your pupil should be from the center of the focal (eye-piece) lens, is usually factory set at four inches. With a clear sight picture, place the intersection of the crosshairs on target and hold steady. If the gun has iron sights, look through the notch in the rear sight and align the front sight blade with it until the blade sits in the rear sight notch flush with its top. Place the aligned sights directly under the target.

Whenever possible, rest the stock forend on a convenient tree branch or other support to help hold it steady. Cowboy shooting is fun in a hay field, but when you might have just one shot to obtain dinner, leave nothing to chance. Rest your gun's weight on any convenient surface that helps to hold it steady and gives you a comfortable, unimpaired shooting position. Do not rest the barrel on anything, only the stock, because the gun's weight, combined with barrel expansion when you fire, will almost certainly make bullets land high.

With your rifle rested and on target, the final, critical step is trigger squeeze. More shots are missed because of a jerked trigger than for any other reason, so the trigger of any rifle (or pistol) must be pulled gently rearward using only the ball of the forefinger, directly opposite the finger-nail and ahead of the first joint. Controlled trigger pull comes with much practice, but novices should never know precisely when their weapon is going to discharge; they should concentrate on holding the sight picture steady on target while gently pulling the trigger until it fires. The discharge should come as a surprise, as does the fact that most beginners who follow these guidelines

RIFLE SIGHTS

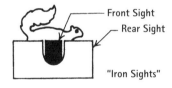

Front Sight
Rear Sight

"Iron Sights"

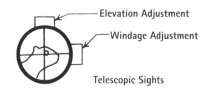

Elevation Adjustment
Windage Adjustment

Telescopic Sights

Rabbits flee until they can no longer see danger, then freeze, sometimes within sight of sharper human vision, which makes them fair game for a survival.

become competent marksmen after only a few shots (presuming, of course, that your gun sights are adjusted to be on target).

Sighting In a Survival Rifle

Weapon sights are merely a guide for their user, a reference point that, ideally, shows where a bullet will land. To reach that point, you first need to adjust the weapon's sights to agree with a bullet's point of impact. Even the best marksman will miss with sights that are out of alignment.

Adjusting a rifle scope to zero, the setting at which crosshairs and bullet impact are in the same place at fifty yards (midrange for the .22 long rifle), requires shooting holes into a target. The technique described here enables almost anyone to mount a scope on a rifle, then zero it with only a few shots. This procedure also allows a scoped rifle to be zeroed in the field, on almost any fixed target, from a standard paper target to a knot on a stump.

First, eliminate any mechanical accuracy problems. All screws used to fasten the scope base to the rifle receiver must be snug; absolutely no movement can occur between rifle and scope. Rings must be fully seated onto their base, and all screws between scope and rings must be snug (check them occasionally). A loose mounting system guarantees that the rifle won't shoot straight, yet this is one of the most common causes of inaccuracy.

The position of a mounted scope should be such that shooters can snap the rifle to their shoulder and see a clear, bright sight picture immediately without moving their head. As mentioned above, eye relief is typically engineered by manufacturers to a standard of four inches.) A scope that is mounted too far forward or rearward presents the shooter with an occluded sight picture that has reduced size and brightness and is surrounded by a dark circle. A properly positioned scope presents a clear, bright sight picture that fills the eyepiece from a comfortable shooting position.

"Your crosshairs are crooked." is a comment you're sure to hear. Ideally, crosshairs should be perfectly vertical and horizontal to a rifle's bore, and the rifle should never be canted in either direction while shooting. In the real world, eyeballing crosshairs to their true position, where a shooter thinks they look straightest, is usually precise enough to head shoot squirrels.

If your bullets consistently land more to the left or right as you adjust the elevation turret upward, then the crosshairs may indeed be cocked to one side. Loosen the ring retaining screws and gently twist the scope barrel until the crosshairs look straight each time you shoulder the gun. To keep the crosshairs in that position, lightly tighten each ring retaining screw a quarter turn at a time until they feel equally snug; called *pattern torquing* by machinists, this procedure ensures that all points of a mounted fixture remain level under pressure.

If your scope appears to be positioned correctly, yet the sight picture looks blurry, the ocular lens—the lens you look through—is probably out of focus. For most scopes, this problem is corrected by loosening the ocular lens's locking ring, just ahead of the eyebell, and turning the entire eyebell (usually) clockwise until the sight picture becomes clear. When maximum clarity has been achieved, secure the ocular lens in that position by turning the locking ring counterclockwise until it presses tightly against the eyebell.

Regardless of caliber, or the range you intend to zero your rifle from, the first three-shot group should be fired from twelve yards, and it should be fired as carefully as if it were from one hundred yards. The rifle forend must be rested solidly, its barrel should touch nothing, and each shot should be aimed precisely at the target's center, regardless of where bullets actually land. Never compensate for a bullet's point of impact by shifting your point of aim and never shoot without a secure rest, because doing either defeats the sighting process.

Using the center of this initial group as a point of reference, remove your scope's turret caps and adjust the windage and elevation knobs to bring the crosshairs into alignment with the point of impact.

Presuming the standard value "1 click = 1/4 inch at 100 yards" (usually marked on the adjusters), crosshairs will move at a rate of thirty-two clicks per inch at twelve yards. If the group's center is 1 inch left of the bull's-eye and 1.5 inches low, adjust the windage (side) turret thirty-two clicks right, and the elevation (top) turret forty-eight clicks upward.

Next, move back to fifty yards and fire another three-shot group. Using the center of that group as a reference, adjust windage and elevation turrets at eight clicks per inch. If the group center is two inches high and one-half inch to the right, adjust sixteen clicks down and four clicks left.

While the above holds true for all scopes marked "1 click equals 1/4 inch at 100 yards," do not expect that it will be exact for all telescopic sights, because all scopes are not created equal. If your rifle is sporting a tactical sight that retails for $1,000, it had better move the point of impact exactly one-fourth inch per click at one hundred yards. But if your gun wears a low-end model that sold for $50 at a department store, it cannot be expected to have the same clockwork precision. An inexpensive scope can get the job done very well once it has been sighted in, but you may have to twist five clicks to equal one inch of movement on a target one hundred yards distant.

Experienced marksmen also recommend making turret adjustments using a procedure known as the *there-and-back* technique. With this method, a shooter who determines that the scope needs, say, four clicks of adjustment will actually turn the turret six clicks in the desired direction, then come back two clicks. This practice is to help ensure that the tiny adjuster gears inside fall into place completely.

If you can't seem to change your bullets' point of impact no matter how many clicks you turn for adjustment, try rapping the scope tube lightly around its turrets with a soft tool (a rubber-handled jackknife works). The delicate inner workings of a telescopic sight can become sticky with time and with exposure to extreme heat and cold, causing the crosshairs inside to hang up. Rapping the turret area gently is usually sufficient to free the mechanism.

Keep scope lenses clean using a soft cloth, like those made for cameras, and keep them covered when not in use. Never use saliva to clean any lens; digestive enzymes in saliva erode the metallic coatings responsible for gathering and transmitting ambient light to a shooter's eye, resulting in a less-vivid sight picture. Treat your telescopic sight well, regardless of its price tag, and it will reward you with years of accurate shooting.

TELESCOPIC RIFLE SCOPE SIGHTING CHART

Yards to target	clicks per inch	one click equals
12.5	32	$1/32$ inch (.031)
25	16	$1/16$ inch (.063)
50	8	$1/8$ inch (.125)
100	4	$1/4$ inch (.250)
150	3	$1/3$ inch (.333)
200	2	$1/2$ inch (.500)
250	1.75	$2/3$ inch (.666)

Yards to target	clicks per inch	one click equals
300	1.50	3/4 inch (.750)
350	1.25	7/8 inch (.875)
400	1	1.0 inch (1.00)

Medical Supplies

Modern medicine accepts that many wild plants have proven medicinal properties, like the antibiotic effect of cudweed or the antihypertensive qualities of Indian poke. The problem is that acquiring an effective field knowledge of herbs, their uses, and how to prepare them as medicine can be a lifelong task in itself. For most people in most survival situations, it's simpler and safer to pack a first-aid kit.

With all respect to the companies that make first-aid kits, no pre-packaged medical kit has yet satisfied me, and I recommend making your own. A homespun first-aid kit won't carry all of those things you never use but are standard for prepackaged outfits. It can have a streamlined collection of tools and medicines that are tailored to a specific environment, season, or even personal needs. Even the pouch, pack, or box you pack it into can be selected to suit particular needs (lots of compartments or pockets are best for segregating items).

Determining what to put into your medical kit is best approached from a perspective of requirements. In summer you probably will not need air-activated heat packs (HotHands, for example) to warm a shock victim's kidney area. In snow country there is little need for antihistamines, analgesic pencils, or other insect bite and allergy medicines. If you are prone to hypoglycemia, glucose tablets may be a lifesaver. If your health depends on a prescription medication, it pays to have a little extra tucked into the medical kit. Again, people who find themselves in real brass tacks survival situations got there with at least some knowledge of what might lie in store, so be prepared.

I got good advice for this chapter from Cheanne Chellis, a working paramedic of twenty years and professional wilderness guide in Michigan's vast Upper Peninsula. Trained in deep-snow

A functional trail survival kit need not be large or heavy to provide the fire, shelter, potable water, and other necessities needed to survive an unplanned night or two in the woods.

and wilderness rescue, she has also taken courses in wilderness first-aid that enable her to convert a typical backpack into an amazing array of medical tools. Cheanne is a comforting presence in the deep woods.

Cuts and Abrasions

Cuts and abrasions on the hands and fingers are the most common injuries in the woods because many survival tasks involve using a sharp edge. The first step is to stop the bleeding, as a wilderness is the wrong place to leak important body fluids. Next, clean and sterilize the wound so that infectious organisms are not trapped inside. The final step is to close the severed edges of the wound, so they can heal together.

For many years, my own cut kit has consisted of a tube of triple antibiotic ointment, three pressure dressings, and several rolls of safety tape in various widths. This medical-grade cotton gauze tape is impregnated with natural latex, which causes it to stick tenaciously to itself but to nothing else, with a grip that holds even when wet. After sterilizing the wound, I wrap several loose (never tight) turns of tape around the finger on either side of the cut, gently pushing the edges almost together. Skin edges should be left slightly apart to permit serum (fluid) drainage as the injury heals from inside first. If bleeding persists, add a pressure bandage, cut to a size that more than covers the wound, and tape it snugly and directly on top to apply constant, localized downward pressure. After about eight hours, I unwind the tape, clean the wound—which has usually stopped bleeding—and apply another looser wrap of safety tape to protect the injury from contamination and bumps. Safety tape has a multitude of other uses too from splinting broken bones, wrapping sprained joints, and immobilizing neck injuries to reattaching a fishing pole's eye, mending a broken snowshoe frame, or wrapping a knife handle to give it a better grip.

The same procedure works with larger appendages, but a gash to the thigh, for example, should initially be closed with butterfly sutures. Essentially, very sticky tape strips that are designed to stick tightly to skin, butterfly sutures are meant to replace stitches for skin-closure applications, but they might not hold a wound closed unless the entire limb is immobilized for at least three days. Even then, do not exert the wounded area or limb more than is absolutely necessary, and immediately stop if you feel so much as a sting from the sutures lest you tear the wound open again.

Do not attempt to suture any wound with needle and thread. Sterile suture kits are available from medical supply outlets for about $6, but few of us have the medical training to reattach flesh, and gangrenous infections have resulted from sealing in infectious agents. Even large open wounds can eventually heal closed without sutures; the primary concern, after you stop the bleeding, is to prevent infection.

The latest in antihemorrhaging agents is a bandage impregnated with, basically, a blend of powdered shrimp shells and vinegar. The active agent in crustacean (and insect) carapaces is called *chitosan*, which becomes ionically attracted to red blood cells when activated by vinegar, causing blood to clot on contact. Marketed under the brand names HemCon and Quick Clot, these bandages can even seal arterial bleeds that would otherwise be fatal in minutes, and they have more than proved themselves in combat. Currently available only to licensed medical professionals (about $60 for a two-inch-by-four-inch piece), these bandages are a must-have for the survival first-aid kit, even if you have to get them from your doctor.

Painkillers

Pain is the body's way of telling you that something is wrong. To use an already injured limb could increase tissue damage, so the brain makes it hurt when you try. Your body wants to be healthy and fit, and pain is just a message for you to slow down until an injury heals. If a person has the choice, he or she should abide by pain messages; never take a painkiller to enable yourself to function with injuries, especially to the spine, or you might turn a minor sprain into a crippling tear.

But pain can also be counterproductive to survival. A throbbing ankle or tooth can keep anyone from getting the restful sleep needed for a body to repair itself, and bedtime is probably the best time to take an analgesic. Ideally, the drug will at least dampen pain without affecting mental faculties or alertness—being hurt in a wilderness is no time to be stoned. Some doctors have OK'd prescription drugs for expeditions, on the condition that they be returned afterward, but for most situations, the best painkillers are available over the counter. Always abide by the manufacturer's directions when taking any drug (people in intense pain can overdose in seeking relief), and use them as sparingly as possible because all have unpleasant long-term effects on internal organs. Do not mix painkillers, because some combinations of even over-the-counter drugs can have harmful effects.

Aspirin

Aspirin is a classic analgesic whose other qualities include thinning the blood and reducing swelling (and throbbing). Aspirin was originally processed from the boiled bark of willows, whose genus name, *Salix*, became the origin of aspirin's chemical name, salicylic acid. This can be useful information to a survivor, because an aspirin, chewed and swallowed, is possibly the most important thing a victim can do at the onset of a suspected heart attack. Aspirin's blood-thinning qualities have also proved valuable for lessening the effects of altitude sickness. Avoid taking aspirin if you are taking other blood-thinning medications, and never give aspirin to a person who is bleeding or suspected to be bleeding internally.

Acetaminophen

Best known under the brand name Tylenol, acetaminophen is a mild painkiller and anti-inflammatory. It is effective for mild sprains, overworked muscles, and headaches but is hard on the kidneys with prolonged use.

Ibuprofen

Once a prescription-only painkiller sold under the name Motrin, ibuprofen is probably the best analgesic pill available for a survival first-aid kit. It is effective at reducing pain as well as swelling and fever. Unlike acetaminophen and aspirin, ibuprofen can be stacked, meaning its pain killing strength can be increased by taking up to five 200 mg tablets at a time. Balance that against the fact that this drug is corrosive to the stomach.

Naproxin Sodium

Another drug that was once prescription only, naproxin sodium is said to have double the painkilling power per milligram as ibuprofen, but that claim is probably more subjective than scientifically quantifiable. In the woods, naproxin sodium has been at least as effective at reducing pain as ibuprofen, and much better than acetaminophen or aspirin.

Supplements

Multivitamin tablets are a required component of a well-stocked wilderness survival medical kit, because a person's best line of defense against illness is his or her own immune system, and healthier people just function better. Many nutrients are bound to be lacking in a diet that comes entirely from nature, and multivitamins are tiny guarantees that your body will receive a recommended dose of most nutrients every day until you run out of them.

But while a good multivitamin can turn a rough meal from nature into a balanced diet, it must be absorbed through the digestive track, and many vitamin pills pass through the colon nearly intact. To obtain maximum absorption, thoroughly chew a multivitamin before swallowing, then wash it down with plenty of water (you'll probably want to do that anyway).

Dental Hygiene

In my book about building and living in an 1800s-style log cabin (*The Log Cabin*, The Lyons Press, 2003), I describe the unfortunate pains encountered while dealing with an abscessed molar, and then, of necessity, extracting it in two parts. The experience sucked, and I do not recommend it.

A toothbrush should be in any survival kit that is intended to keep its owner alive for more than a day. Like everything, the best method of dealing with dental issues is to keep them from occurring in the first place, and regular brushing, even without toothpaste is said to be enough to clean away plaque and prevent gum disease. Some travel toothbrushes fit into their own handles to form a package that is (ironically) about the size of a pack of gum.

Teeth and gums can also be cleaned with a twig brush, made by chewing the end of an usually astringent green twig—like witch hazel or willow—until it becomes fibrous like a coarse brush. The brush can be used to gently scrub clean teeth and gums, dislodging particles that might cause a problem, and doing a surprisingly good job, even on back teeth.

Survival First-Aid Kits

Whether transported in a breast pocket or strapped on to an air boat, the objective of a survival first-aid kit is to give its owner as many medical options and capabilities as can be fitted into an easily carried container. Options for containment and carrying are numerous, from simply dedicating one pocket of a parka shell to belt pouches to segregated plastic boxes to the comprehensive orange day pack medical kit I toss into the truck or boat for multi-day trail- or river-running trips. The canvas-bag jump kit in paramedic Cheanne's personal truck is even more extensive, including a blood pressure cuff, wraparound SAM splints (handy in the backwoods), a stethoscope, even IV kits.

How large or comprehensive your own kit will be depends on how it will be carried, but exercise the same pragmatic "it's gotta work" approach that you would to any kit in a survival outfit. You can equip a kit to the point of its being unwieldy, so here are a few of the generic cornerstones of working field medical kits:

Generic First-Aid Kit Items

1 tube antibiotic ointment
1 roll one-inch wide safety tape
Butterfly sutures, assorted sizes
1 bottle ibuprofen (or naproxin sodium) tablets
1 package glucose tablets (for hypoglycemia)
1 bottle aspirin
1 bottle multivitamins
10 Micropur MP1 water purification tablets
10 Benadryl (diphenhydramine) antihistamine capsules
10 loperamide hydrochloride antidiarrheal caplets
1 one-liter water bottle
1 tube liquid hand soap
6 alcohol prep pads
1 pair toenail clippers

1 pair tweezers
1 small pair scissors
1 toothbrush
1 two-inch-by-4-inch chitosan clotting bandage
1 package sewing needles, assorted sizes
EMS Field Guide (Informed Publishing, 2006)

Water Treatments

With better knowledge, many of the accepted facts about wilderness survival—and everything else—have proved to be in error. When I was a kid, iodine tablets were touted to kill all infectious organisms, and we used them or tincture of iodine (four drops per quart) with the hope that we were protected from parasites that everyone seemed to get anyway. In the early 1980s, the American Centers for Disease Control (CDC) discovered that *Giardia lamblia*, a parasitic flagellate, was ubiquitous in natural waters—no stream was safe to drink from without first treating its water. Next came the recognition of *Cryptosporidium parvum*, a parasitic intestinal cyst, that the CDC today estimates will infect 80 percent of North Americans at least once in their lifetime. Near the turn of the century it was learned that iodine, my trusted shield against parasites for more than thirty years, did not kill *Cryptosporidium parvum*, or the lesser known cyclospora cyst—which explains why I and so many of my camping companions suffered bouts of dysentery, fever, and nausea that everyone just attributed to "some kind of bug." The U.S. National Park Service has warned that tapeworm eggs washed by rain into the ponds of Lake Superior's Isle Royale National Park might infect hikers who drink untreated water.

It is never in the best interest of any parasite to kill its host—and probably itself—so most invaders are not fatal to most victims. In fact, many parasites are ingested and pass through the victim without gaining a foothold, depending on the intended victim's constitution (some people are actually immune) and the number of organisms ingested. Species differ, but typically the animal or egg is swallowed by drinking water from lakes or streams that are always fed by runoff, sometimes from many miles inland, which washes over scats (dung) that carry the next generation of a parasitic species. Immune to digestive juices, the organism begins, and sometimes stays, in a colony within the digestive tract where the sustenance needed to reproduce is stolen from the host. At cycle's end, usually about two months, the parasite and its offspring are excreted in solid waste to wait for the next rain or snowmelt. A healthy host will live through the infestation with periodic bouts of fever, diarrhea, and general flulike symptoms. The danger comes when the host is already under stress that saps his or her resources—diabetes, malnutrition, even a head cold—and unpleasant symptoms of the infestation open the door for other ills.

Boiling

Every day pack or larger survival kit needs a mess kit for boiling water (and cooking) because boiling is a sure-fire method of killing every organism in a pot of water. The old GI canteen-and-cup outfit was ideal for making water potable on the trail; just boil untreated water in the cup over a fire, let it cool to tepid, and pour the safe water into the canteen. Today my trail survival kits carry a European-style military one-liter pot with lid, nested dish, and a spoon whose handle is bent into a hook for snagging the pot's wire handle from a hot fire. Inside the kit carries Ramen noodles or other boilables, usually coffee or tea to stave off caffeine-withdrawal headaches. If you don't have a cooking vessel available, any discarded metal can, even a glass bottle, can suffice to boil water over a fire. It is possible to boil water in a plastic container if the fire is low and the bottle is kept filled with water.

Water boils at 212 degrees Fahrenheit at sea level. Nearly every harmful organism dies before the temperature reaches 180 degrees, but you don't need a cooking thermometer to see a rolling boil. Two minutes of boiling is sufficient to ensure the demise every living thing. At higher altitudes—and even at sea level—it helps to weight the lid of a cook pot with a stone to convert it into a pressure cooker

Boiling water for two minutes is enough to guarantee the demise of all organisms in it, but it does not reduce chemical or metal contaminants.

of sorts. Bear in mind that boiling cannot reduce the presence of chemicals or heavy metals.

Boiling also cannot reduce the volume of sediment in natural waters, and these particulates can make water viscous enough to induce gagging, even if it has been boiled safe. A basic solution to this problem is to prefilter water by covering the mouth of your container with woven cloth before you fill it. A handkerchief—always recommended as outdoor wear—is fine enough to strain out objectionable particles, but almost any piece of woven clothing works.

The Seepage Well

A survival skill to delight the purist, the seepage well is merely a smaller variation of the hand-dug village "wishing" well that provided water to almost every community until the nineteenth century. By digging a hole down to the water table, a pool of essentially spring water could be formed at its bottom where no harmful organisms could get to. So long as the well pit was kept free of drowned mice and runoff by a surrounding wall and from bird guano by a pitched roof, water that seeped into its bottom was safe for drinking. To the dismay of early firefighters, a seepage well can be scooped dry, taking a full day or so to refill, but this also enabled contaminated wells to be emptied and cleaned.

In a survival situation, seepage wells are best dug in a fresh-water shoreline, preferably sand, and at least four feet from the water's edge. Top layers of soil are almost guaranteed to harbor some organisms, so sweep them far back from the well pit's edge as you dig. You will hit water at the same level as the water lapping the shoreline, but continue excavating until you have a pool that is filling with water even as you dig. It is important to have several inches of water at the bottom to permit scooping it out without stir-ring silt at the bottom. Water seeping into the hole is safe to drink immediately, but you might want to wait until it has settled. A seep-age well can serve a survivor indefinitely, permitting one to make camp on any shoreline without fear of waterborne parasites. Desert survivors should be warned that if a pool is poisoned from alkali or chemicals, water seeping into the hole will likely be poisoned too.

Chemical Water Purifiers

Iodine and chlorine (halazone) destroy bacteria, viruses, and giardia, but not cysts like cryptosporidium. Tablets made from sodium chlo-rite and sodium dichloroisocyanurate dihydrate, like the Micropur MP1 tablets from Katadyn, have made iodine and chlorine obsolete as water treatments. Each Micropur tab treats one liter of water, killing giardia, bacteria, and viruses within fifteen minutes, but it requires a four-hour wait to ensure the demise of tough cysts. Simi-lar to the Micropur tablets are the new electrochemical purifiers, for example, MiOx from MSR. These gizmos use watch batteries to electrify a chamber filled with raw water and rock salt, converting those elements to chemicals that are safe for humans but deadly to pathogenic organisms. According to MSR staff microbiologist Lisa Lange, the superoxygenated solution is a cocktail of antimicrobial chemicals that will kill all organisms within a liter of water, although a four-hour wait time is needed to ensure the elimination of cysts.

Because these purifiers can quickly treat large volumes of water, they have become almost standard for disaster-relief operations.

Water Filters

Survival instructors have said that it is better to drink untreated water than to risk dehydration. It's best to avoid both of those problems; a seepage well (described above) accomplishes that, but the most convenient and the quickest for on-trail use is the hiking water filter. Regulated by the EPA to make wild water safe to drink, these units typically employ a two-stage pump action to draw raw water into the suction chamber then force that water through a filter where anything larger than a virus is removed. Potable water on the opposite side of the filter is directed through an output hose. Most of these filters can treat hundreds of gallons before filter replacement is necessary; weighing about one pound and about as big as an aerosol can, most units fit into a pocket.

All water filters must perform under federal safety standards, but not all of them are the same. Based on more than a decade of

Collapsible water bladders roll up to fit into a pocket, but they can transport more than a gallon of water.

field trials with more than a dozen models, paper filter cartridges, like Katadyn's Hiker model, are good to at least their (usually) two-hundred-gallon rating, depending on the siltiness of the water being filtered, but they eventually have to be replaced. Ceramic cartridges, like the one used by MSR's combat-proven WaterWorks filter, clog more quickly and need cleaning with nearly every use, but filters are easily wiped clean, and you will probably never need another—just be careful not to drop a ceramic filter onto a hard surface because it can break.

Prices for a dependable paper cartridge water filter begin at around $60, with replacement cartridges running at about half that. Ceramic filter units start at under $100, with high-end, high-performance models reaching to several hundred dollars, and replacement cartridges, again, cost about half the unit price.

Miscellaneous Items

If portability permits, a survival outfit can, and should, be expanded beyond the hard-core basics to include other tools for making daily

If your transport into a wilderness allows—be it a helicopter, pickup truck, or kayak—there is no reason not to have that vehicle equipped to provide for foreseeable needs.

life easier in an unforgiving place. A geocaching enthusiast might be restricted to just carrying the fundamentals, but there is no reason for snowmobilers not to have a bag of tricks for surviving any blizzard while strapped on to their machine. Probably none of the following items will be critical to survival, but all of them have proved their worth under field conditions.

Spare Socks

During the sometimes vicious winters of the Korean War, many casualties were caused by cold, with frostbite, trench foot, and other foot ailments topping the list of injuries that took soldiers out of action. Dry spare socks made from wool in those days were considered a battlefield survival item. As I heard it, "Dry socks are much more important than clean underwear."

Far advanced beyond the abrasive woolies of yesteryear, synthetic-knit socks today shed moisture to help prevent blisters and retain warmth, provide padding to allow a more secure fit between foot and boot, and help to cushion the footbed. All these qualities help to keep a hiker's feet from aching at day's end—one less distraction while doing other tasks.

Gloves

I always advise survival students to bring along a pair of noninsulated leather work gloves for a class. The fibrous stalks of bracken ferns—used for shelter covering and padding—can slice flesh like a jagged razor, working around fire is a lot safer with a shield of leather between hands and flames, breaking dead limbs from a shelter support can lacerate hands, and gloves can provide added security for some knife work. They also help to prevent the machete-caused blisters that are almost a feature of survival classes. Retailing for around $10 per pair, leather glove shells are an inexpensive safeguard for your ultimate survival tools—your hands. You can learn to pull a trigger and tie knots while wearing them, and stretchy knit acrylic liners (about $1 per pair in the kids' department) increases the shells' warmth rating to about twenty degrees Fahrenheit.

Hats

In open country, especially the desert, a wide-brimmed hat is survival gear, a vital source of shade to protect the eyes from glare, an umbrella in the rain, and even a bowl or bucket if the situation demands it. I've used my own hats to filter silt from cooking water, even to catch minnows as fish bait. In cold country, where a jacket hood may be required to fend off subzero windchills, brimmed hats are likely to be billed caps, which can accommodate a hood better and still shade the eyes from glare that might cause temporary snow blindness. Like other clothing, the preferred hats are made from synthetic materials or wool (not cotton) to better dissipate perspiration. Prices for hats vary from a couple of dollars to outrageous amounts, but survivalists should make a hat part of their outfit in every season.

Slingshots

Usually equated with adolescent ruffians, elastic-band slingshots have accounted for a lot of wild game dinners over the generations. First came bands of tire inner tubes attached to a Y-shaped stick and connected by a rawhide projectile pouch. The old Y-shape delinquent's slingshot is also effective for launching fishing arrows. More powerful and more accurate is the tube-frame Wrist Rocket type slingshot that uses latex tubing as the power band and is available for about $10 at sporting goods counters. Able to use even rocks as ammo, the slingshot can fling any suitable projectile with aimed, lethal force capable of killing small game—if a shooter has the marksmanship (I've never shown talent with a slingshot).

Dog Rag

Named during the Vietnam War, the dog rag is essentially an oversize cotton handkerchief that served a multitude of purposes, many survival related. It could be a washcloth, towel, sweat band, tourniquet, bandage, filter, or face mask. Being cotton, it could absorb rain for drinking water, carry smaller items in a bindle, or wipe down a rifle. Considering the huge number of uses for a simple square of cloth, it's a good idea to carry at least one handkerchief all the time.

Radio Receiver

Even when I was a kid it made no sense to leave behind my five-transistor AM-only pocket radio when I went to the woods. Its nine-volt battery life was a dismal four hours (if I kept it warm), and the technology of weather forecasting was much less precise than it is today, but that receiver frequently provided a valuable warning about fast-moving storm fronts. In fact, a more advanced portable receiver, when I was deep in the woods, informed me of the awful news about the terrorist attacks on the World Trade Center. For survivors, a radio receiver provides a soul-warming reminder of the outside world that awaits their return, as well as perhaps useful local news about rescue efforts concerning them.

Many radio receivers have passed through my survival outfits over the years, from crank-charged "cabin" radios that are too big to carry to card-size AM-FM models you might forget are in your pocket. Today every camping trip I plan includes a multi-band AM-FM-shortwave receiver. Powered by AA rechargeable lithium ion batteries (which can be charged in the field with my Brunton Solaris folding solar panel), these receivers are typically the size of a small paperback, and many deliver more than thirty hours of service on a set of batteries. And even though modern portables receive stations from around the world, prices begin at less than $75.

Sewing Kit

A sewing kit can make survival less of a pain. You can reattach buttons, repair torn pockets, or otherwise fix damaged clothing, cloth gear, and straps; without it, you might be hard put to do any of those things. A working sewing kit, whose real value far outweighs its cost, containing a small spool of nylon thread, a dozen needles of various sizes (for cloth to canvas), and several spare buttons will fit into a plastic pill bottle. Total cost is about $3.

Bug-Fighting Outfit

A malady common to northern lumberjacks, especially novices, of the 1800s was swamp madness, an often psychotic condition that caused them to go insane, sometimes violently. The "disease" usually passed after the victim had been moved back to town for a few days, because it was actually a nervous breakdown caused by long days of hard labor in swarms of biting flies combined with sleepless nights of endless torment by mosquitoes. Some adapted (the human body possesses some repellent qualities in skin oils), while others worked at a sawmill in town. For a winter survival kit, or one tailored to an environment where biting insects are not a concern, this section has no application. But if your kit is engineered for the many places where clouds of biting insects fly into eyes, nose, and mouth, and stab into any skin they can reach—even through denim—then read on.

The Enemies

Mosquitoes are only one family of biting bugs you might have to deal with. Worldwide, there are more than three hundred species of horsefly and deerfly (family *Tabanidae*) and six hundred species of blackfly (family *Simuliidae*). All are determined biters, especially when they hatch in the millions and form clouds, and they can pose a very real danger to humans and animals. A blackfly that zooms into your eyeball can cause an involuntary reaction that causes you to fall, but maybe most important is the potential for an allergic reaction to the anticoagulant venom that all bloodsuckers inject into victims. Itchy bites are a torment, but enough of them can send a victim into anaphylactic shock (here's where the Benadryl capsules in your first-aid kit come in). Deaths aren't limited to humans, at the peak of their population cycles flies have been known to remove more than a pint of blood per day from domestic animals, and thousands of animals are said to die each year from insect bites.

Deerflies and Horseflies

These tabanids are the strongest of the bloodsucking fliers, and probably everyone recognizes the deerfly as the insect that entangles

Properly equipped in the New Millennium, canoeists and kayakers can penetrate the wildest, most remote backwaters with relative impunity.

itself in your hair. A deerfly's preferred target is the creases in the finger joints where even a quick bite causes stinging and swelling that lasts for hours. Up to four times larger than the housefly-size deerfly, horseflies are seldom successful at biting humans, but when they succeed, their razorlike proboscis often leaves a freely bleeding gash that stings for a day. A handy tip to know about deerflies and horseflies is that they like open sky overhead and do not enter covered enclosures—including tents.

Blackflies
Blackflies usually hatch before mosquitoes, in April or May, and the sight of millions of these tiny demons rising in black clouds from a beaver pond is enough to cause dread in a seasoned woods-

DEERFLY

BLACKFLY

man. The bite is normally painless but bleeds freely and is followed by a dime-size wheal that itches intensely for several days. At peak season, blackflies attack mindlessly, driving into every exposed orifice. This fly has been known to kill thousands of animals in a single season and humans exposed to them have sometimes required hospitalization. Fortunately, blackflies also do not enter roofed enclosures, so relief can be found inside a tent or shelter.

Mosquitoes

The three main genera of mosquitoes, or biting crane flies, are *Aedes*, *Culex*, and *Anopheles*, and all are found in North America. With a few exceptions, such as West Nile virus, people living north of Mexico don't generally worry about mosquito-borne diseases, although the worst outbreak of yellow fever in U.S. history occurred in New York at the end of the nineteenth century. Even so, from the start of their hatch in May or June until the autumn cold ends their activity, mosquitoes can be a ceaseless torment, day and night. Unlike other biting flies, mosquitoes have no fear of entering enclosures, so you cannot escape them inside a shelter. Mosquitoes do not like bright sunlight, preferring to keep to shadows, but sunshine is the realm of other biting flies.

Insect Repellents

Humans have always sought a magic shield that will keep bugs from biting. The idea of a chemical repellent probably began with the practice of tucking a sprig of bergamot (horsemint) into a hat band or a chrysanthemum into a buttonhole, both of which are repulsive to mosquitoes. Today a multitude of sprays and lotions are available, even butane-powered gizmos that emit heated chemical fumes.

Currently the chemical known by the acronym DEET is the standard for personal bug protection. It's available in spray or lotion, and judged safe for use on bare skin—although it will dissolve some types of polystyrene plastic.

Manufactured cocktails of natural bug-repelling ingredients, like eucalyptus and spearmint, have proved to be as effective in the field as DEET-based products. A bottle of Green Ban lotion has been a fixture in my own summer outfits for nearly a decade.

Clothing repellent sprays containing pyrethrin (a natural derivative from the chrysanthemum family) or permethrin (synthesized pyrethrin) are widely used in flea sprays, livestock sprays, and other applications that do not come into contact with human skin. Clothing treated with either add a valuable layer of repellency against flying insects but also against ticks, chiggers, and other mites. Maybe best of all, permethrin tends to remain in cloth fibers for more than three days, so clothing can be pretreated before an outing. Larger survival kits in bug country should carry a spray bottle of the stuff for periodic refreshing.

The bottom line on every bug repellent, including natural repellents and even campfire smoke, is that a new hatch of bugs is so insanely driven to get the blood meal needed to lay viable eggs that I believe they would bite if you were on fire. When mosquitoes or blackflies fill the air in numbers so great that they literally bump one another to get to you, repellents get little notice from them.

Natural Insect Repellents

Nature provides a few of its own repellents. The first line of defense is knowing that all biting insects need moisture to breed; mosquitoes require standing water (they can even spawn in an old rain-filled coffee can), but stable flies (biting houseflies that go for the ankles) and deerflies need only wet, decaying vegetation to hatch. Wet, windless places in the deep forest are likely to be awful in summer, so it pays to keep to higher, breezier ground while traveling. When camping, smoke generated from a hot bed of coals that is fed damp, rotting wood or armfuls of green bracken ferns will eventually drive away all bugs, if you generate enough of it long enough.

Sleeping next to a low, smoky fire on a foliage-padded pallet of body-length dead branches laid parallel to one another provides some protection from bugs to let you get restful sleep. During heavy bug hatches, you might opt to surround your camp with a number of small "smudge" fires whose only purpose is to make smoke from wet leaves or rotting wood.

On the trail you will find plants that generate natural insect repellents like pyrethrin to protect themselves from plant-eating insects. Some of the best and most common plant repellents are

BLOODROOT

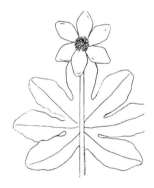

Blooms late spring to fall. White flower in front of single blue-green leaf. Grows up to ten inches in height. Red sap from root and stem can be applied to skin as an insect repellant.

CATNIP

Mint family. Blooms from early summer to early fall in moist, rich soil. Flower heads clustered, ranging from white to pale violet. Leaves contain an oil toxic to insects.

COMMON TANSY

WILD LEEK

Summer Flower

Spring Growth Form

Blooms in late summer with clusters of small yellow ray flowers. Plant may be more than five feet tall, but two feet is normal. Juice of entire plant repels all insects. Toxic if eaten.

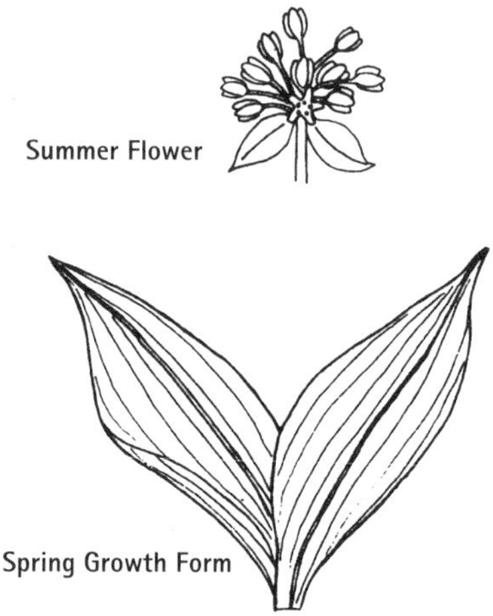

Member of onion family. Strong-smelling edible bulb. Flowers white to pink. Juice of entire plant repels insects.

shown in the illustrations on p. 55 and above. To use any of them, crush and roll the plant's leaves and flowers between your palms until it becomes a wet green mass, then squeeze the repellent-containing juices into one palm and apply to areas that need protection.

In the absence of insect repellent, a survivalist can get protection by covering the face, hands, and other exposed areas with a layer of mud. Clothing should be buttoned as snugly as possible around the wrists and neck, and trouser legs should be bloused or tied securely at the ankles. Biting insects aren't the only reason for this security; I've had yellowjackets sting my ankles multiple times after crawling up my pant leg.

The Indispensable Head Net

When biting insects refuse to respect repellents and you just have to live with them, a simple bag-shaped head net made from no-see-um netting and worn over a brimmed hat or ball cap can be a sanity saver. I sewed these invaluable bug stoppers from netting (even lace curtains) for many years, but now they can be purchased ready made for about $5. By keeping airborne attackers from diving into eyes and facial orifices and from getting to soft spots, a head net worn in combination with long sleeves and trousers lets you tolerate bug populations that would likely drive an unprotected person's mind out of reality and maybe make one sick. When not in use protecting your sanity, a head net can serve as a water prefilter, as a carry sack for smoked meat and dried foods that keep best when air circulates around them, and even as a fishing net. For hunting, a head net made from camouflage-print netting can make its wearer's head disappear while still permitting enough visibility to see crosshairs in a rifle scope. When not in use, the head net rolls up and stashes in the corner of a pocket.

Recommended Items for the Survival Kit

No survival kit will provide for every contingency in every environment, but the following items are generic to all conditions. Some of these things are not feasible for pockets, so folks who just want to see where a trail goes can get by with the basic three (map and compass, knife, and fire starter) described on pp. 2–14 at the beginning of this book. For all-day hikes (and backcountry travel of all kinds) I carry a day-and-a-half backpack, like the Exponent Otero, which provides room for bivy shelter, a bedroll, water filter and bottle, metal cup, food, and comforts sufficient to keep nearly any bad situation from looking hopeless. I believe this piece of life insurance is worth its fifteen-pound carry weight should something go wrong when help is far away.

The following list represents some of the most current and best survival gear on the market today. Membership in this group means that the named item has endured real field use long enough and in all types of applicable weather to be trusted. A few have received the hard-won Best Buy award, (admittedly, given by me) in *Consumers Digest* magazine. Products mentioned by name should be seen as

At just twenty-five pounds, this survival pack carries everything two people need to survive indefinitely in any season.

examples of acceptable quality, because some manufacturers discontinue models as fast as they introduce new ones. Bear in mind that none of the survival kit contents given here are written in stone, and you should add to them as needed to suit different environments. Also, you will notice that some items are duplicated as you step up in terms of equipment and the ability to handle more problems. NASA has always known the value of redundancy and backup systems in an environment where little problems can have big consequences, and the same approach applies to practical wilderness survival.

Survival Knife Kit
(attached to your trousers except when sleeping)
Knife, strong, sharp: Ontario Knife RAT-7 D2 Steel, Mission Knives MPK10 (titanium)

Sheath: secure snap-down retainer, thigh tie-down, large
cargo pouch
Compass, pocket: Silva Type 7, Brunton Tag-A-Long
Fire starter: U.S. Survival Strike Force, U.S. Survival Blast
Match

Pocket Survival Kit (these things never leave your person)

Compass: Coleman 3-in-1 compass/whistle/match case,
Brunton 11HNL with whistle
Map: trail or topographical, preferably laminated with clear
contact paper
Folding knife, pocket clip: Columbia River M21, Benchmade
RUKUS
Fire starter: butane lighter, Strike Force flint and steel, waxed
cotton string fire wicks
First-aid kit (in ziplock bag): roll of one-inch safety tape,
tube of triple antibiotic ointment
Space blanket or disposable painter's drop cloth

Survival Parka Shell (also includes all of the above)

Parka shell, hooded, many pockets, waterproof, ventilated:
Columbia Titanium
Orienteering compass: Brunton SightMaster, Brunton 8099
Eclipse
Folding multifunction tool: Gerber Multitool, Buck BuckTool,
Leatherman
Fire starter: butane lighter, Strike Force flint and steel, tinder
Cord: at least fifteen feet of military-issue parachute cord
Gloves, leather shell: Wells Lamont
Fishing kit (in pill bottle): hooks, sinkers, at least twenty feet
of strong fishing line
Snacks: High-carb, one thousand calories, for fending off
hypoglycemia

Water bladder: one liter, MSR Platypus

Water purification tabs: Katadyn MicroPur MP-1

Flashlight: Mini-Maglite AA-cell LED, Petzl AAA LED head-lamp with strobe mode

Signal mirror, lightweight, with sighting hole: U.S. Survival Star Flash

Survival Day Pack, All-Day Carry
(also includes all of the above)

Day pack, many pockets, padded, adjustable harness: Exponent Otero, Kelty Bison (camouflage)

Compass and map

GPS (optional)

Heavy machete (strapped on to pack): Ontario Knife SP-8, Ka-Bar Cutlass Machete

Shelter, bivy type, compact: Exponent Kraz X1, Integral Designs Mega Sola

Water filter: Katadyn Hiker, MSR WaterWorks II

Water bladder: Platypus two liter

Sleeping bag, ultralight mummy, synthetic fill, rated about twenty degrees: Exponent Canyon

Sleeping pad: Therm-A-Rest Pro-Lite 3 (inflatable), Therm-A-Rest Z-Lite (closed-cell foam)

First-aid kit: packed in its own case, comprehensive— dysentery, pain, bleeding, allergies, sprains, and so on

Fire starters: butane lighter, matches, waxed-cotton fire wicks, military trioxane tabs

Cord: GI 550-pound parachute cord, fifty feet or more

Cord: nylon packaging string, fifty-yard spool

Socks, synthetic knit, padded: SmartWool, WigWam

Radio receiver, AM-FM-SW: Kaito KA1102

Cook set, lightweight, designed for boiling: European military surplus cook pot set, MSR Titan Mini Cookset

Cup, metal, about one pint: Coleman/Peak 1, MSR Titan titanium cup

Spoon, teaspoon with metal handle bent backward into a hook for snagging hot handles from fire

Food, nonperishable, 6,000 calories (three days) per person: granola bars, rice, raisins, chocolate, and so on

Frog gig spearhead, three prongs, carried with points safely embedded in foam or other suitable material

Slingshot, folding, latex tubing, wrist brace

As shown by the fleece shirt and jacket hanging from backpack straps, a layered outfit is adjustable to prevent overheating during periods of exertion, and this principle should be applied to outdoor clothing in every season or environment.

Optional Items for the Survival Kit

What you need and how important an item might be to survival depends very much on random chance. If you're suffering a dizzy spell from hypoglycemia while hiking a rocky ledge, getting blood sugars back to operating levels can be imperative. If you find yourself in a cold, drenching rain, making a fire may save your life. In desert country water becomes critical. And if you're far from civilization when you encounter a large, rabid raccoon or coyote (not uncommon in the spring), you will probably want a gun—even if you aren't normally much into firearms. Since you can't predict what might have life-saving value, it pays to prepare for as many contingencies as you can, and those needs will not always be the same. Presuming you know roughly where you will be, if a situation comes up that requires survival techniques you can prepare ahead to live indefinitely under whatever conditions you might encounter.

Outfitted for a week of comfortable backpacking in one of America's wildest regions, this EMT-certified survival instructor has his own needs covered, as well as those of his clients, all in a backpack that weighs fifty pounds.

What Do I Do First?

It's safe to say that few people who are thrust into a do-or-die survival situation will be in a clear state of mind, particularly if there are injuries involved. We Homo sapiens are exceptionally capable when it comes to adapting to and taking from the environment to suit our needs, but the same big brain that enables us to do that also makes us able to envision a thousand horrible fates. We don't just live in the moment like other animals, but we consider future possibilities, and the dark side of imagination is fear. Fight or flight works for creatures adapted to face attacks that are simple and direct, but panic does not work for a hairless, toolless biped who naturally possesses almost none of the physical endowments needed to survive on this planet. Being afraid is inevitable when you know that just staying alive might be challenging for the indefinite future, but there are many well-established reasons to fear the effects of panic more than any potential dangers.

The opposite of panic is logic, and the first thing to do in any survival situation, whether it's a plane crash in the Canadian Rockies or just a busted ATV in the middle of nowhere, is to take stock of what you have. The exercise is necessary to determine what you are going to need to make camp or hike home, and it forces the brain into a problem-solving mode. This too stimulates imagination, but as you use a compass and map to determine where you are, and especially after you've made a warm fire, the visions that come to you are likely to be positive. Instead of being fearful of the entire situation, you will begin to dissect individual problems and obstacles, overcoming them in order of importance, and in doing so, you will almost inevitably find that there are many options for getting through your situation.

Opinions vary, but my philosophy is that you are your own best chance at surviving a tough situation, and unless you're stranded by injuries or dangerous terrain, your best bet is to hike for the nearest road—usually less than a day's walk in most places. If the problem is that your vehicle is trapped by trees fallen across the trail after a storm (it happens), just shouldering the survival day pack described earlier virtually guarantees that you have the means to survive a three-day march in any weather. Lacking a proper survival kit, scavenge whatever useful and transportable tools might be available; for every hike you will need water, and an empty soda bottle will suffice. Spare butane lighters, candies and foods, and other potentially useful but transportable items should be pocketed. Unless you have indeed gone naked into the woods, even the most unprepared survivor will discover that by employing a little ingenuity and a few proven survival techniques, there are more options than were apparent at first glance.

When hiking out (see chapter 6), it pays to avoid some of the more common mistakes. An important realization is that the length of a mile can be very subjective; in open country where visibility stretches to the horizon, a mile passes quickly. In the forest, where every step brings a new unfamiliar vista and visibility is measured in feet, miles pass more slowly, and it is common to overestimate how far one has traveled. Pinballing from one obvious mapped landmark to another provides reassurance that you know where you're headed and helps to quell doubts about whether you missed a turn. Check your compass frequently while hiking to ensure that you are following the correct bearing; no one likes to accept it, but humans can become completely turned around in less than a hundred yards. Likewise, refrain from doubting your compass and especially from making intuitive course corrections; a working compass cannot be wrong or inaccurate, it can only point toward the magnetic north pole.

When hiking back to civilization, do not punish yourself. A desire to get home or to get help for an injured companion can cause you to push too hard. Abraded hot spots on your feet will be healed by morning if you stop and dry your feet and socks right away, but if you force them to become blisters, every step will be a lesson in pain for the next week. Sore back muscles can adjust to overland travel if you ease them through the transition, but if you push them until one tears, the injury can literally cripple you for weeks.

If a situation demands staying put until someone finds you, the same philosophy of self-kindness applies. Make yourself at home; build a fire and make sure everyone present is as warm, hydrated, and well fed as conditions permit. Within a day or so, the piece of wilderness you occupy will naturally begin to transform into a camp, with shelter, fire, work spaces, even trails. Medical complications aside, a lame canoeist whose vessel has been mangled in a rapid, or in a similar disabling disaster, should be capable of surviving indefinitely just with what is in the person's pockets.

TWO

Survival Shelters

Shelter building has been an essential part of human existence for as long as our species has been here, and the instinct can still be seen in toddlers who crawl inside cardboard boxes or in the fun a group of children can have building a fort. We are probably born with an urge to be sheltered, but few people have needed to actually build one to survive in a wilderness in many generations, and the nuts-and-bolts mechanics of shelter construction have not been a component of normal life in a very long time.

Even so, people around the world have demonstrated that every environment provides the materials to build shelter. Rock, sod, wood, animal hides, even snow, have all been transformed into sheltering walls and roofs—in fact, without a transportable tent (the tepee), human migration across glaciers might have been impossible. There is no place where a survivor cannot find or build shelter from materials found in the environment.

The Need for Shelter

Often underestimated, especially in the American West where sleeping under the stars is part of the outdoor experience, shelter is vital to long-term survival everywhere. One critic faulted the first edition of this book for focusing too much on the dangers of hypothermia, probably because I "hail from the north woods," as he put it. But that only tells me that this guy is an RV camper. Even at the equator, a storm with wind and rain can reduce felt temperatures to near freezing and kill or seriously sicken an unprotected human in just hours. The importance of shelter is probably best demonstrated by the fact that villages of permanent or seasonal houses are a hallmark of every human culture at every latitude.

An effective primitive shelter must meet roughly the same requirements as a house, which are essentially to provide a shell whose interior is always warm, dry, and comfortable, regardless of the weather outside. It has a bed above the earth, padded and insulated, with exterior roof and walls that seal out rain and drafts, trapping as much warm dead air inside as possible. As with everything about wilderness survival, there are many options for accomplishing those goals.

Wearable Shelters

Of the roughly one hundred deaths that occur in North America's wilderness each year, most are attributable to hypothermia and to infectious germs and viruses that get a foothold once the immune system has been depressed by cold. Remember, any ambient temperature lower than our body temperature is stealing heat from us, and the cooling effect increases dramatically with rain and wind. Being chilled to the bone because you didn't have enough sense to come in from the rain and caught your death of pneumonia are a few clichés that demonstrate how much cold and its effects were feared by American settlers, even south of the snow line. Despite their claims, today's outdoorsmen are not as tough as the nineteenth-century homesteaders, nor are any of us as experienced at primitive living, but we do have another century's worth of knowledge and technology that permits us to survive in outer space, a mile underwater, and even in foul weather. The bottom line is that there is simply no good excuse for a modern outdoorsman—including paying clients who are just along for the ride or flight—to suffer from hypothermia.

Dressing warmly is not rocket science, but it is a science, and anyone who wants to actually enjoy being in stormy weather should be familiar with the thermodynamics of layering with today's high-efficiency synthetic fabrics. There are essentially three layers in a foul weather outfit: A base layer (long underwear) is first, worn in direct contact with the skin, followed by an intermediate layer (which may be two or three layers), and finally, a tough, weatherproof outer shell. Each of these layers performs a specific function that is different from yet complements the others, and each component needs to be easily removable to facilitate mixing and matching layers in changing weather conditions.

First, and this is optional in warm temperatures, is the base layer or long johns. This layer captures an atmosphere of warmed, motionless dead air over the wearer's skin to retain body heat. Yet it must breathe well enough to allow swift dissipation of perspiration vapors and at the same time absorb as little moisture as possible. Cotton in any amount is a bad choice because it sucks up and holds moisture (like a towel), displacing insulating dead air with cooling wetness, and it dries slowly, subjecting its wearer to constant cooling from evaporation. Duofold's ThermaStat fabric and Medalist's very warm X-Static are as good as wool at dissipating moisture while retaining body heat. Base layer sets (top and bottoms) made from synthetics or wool retail for around $40. When not needed, the set can be stuffed into a jacket pocket.

For the legs, densely-woven nylon six-pocket overpants ($50) worn over base-layer bottoms are rugged enough for any terrain but stop heat-stealing wind. In double-digit subzero temps I add a second base-layer bottom sized large enough to fit loosely over the first. Wool works well here, shielded from the skin by a softer synthetic layer. Six-pocket Gore-Tex overpants (about $80) are great for cold rain or snow, and I've always liked German army surplus double-wall heavyweight wool trousers (about $40) for multiday winter outings.

The intermediate layer, which might actually be two or more layers depending on activity levels and temperature, is worn over the base layer. Its job is to inhibit loss of body heat from the base layer by providing additional layers of warmed air while also conducting moisture vapors outward. Synthetic fleece, preferably with a zip turtleneck, is ideal for this layer, but so is an old-fashioned knitted wool sweater.

Covering the base and intermediate layers is an noninsulated windproof and waterproof parka shell, preferably with a detachable hood. The jacket is unlined because layers beneath provide insulation; the shell only prevents body heat from being whisked away by wind or washed away by rain. That function is important: A snowmobiler riding thirty-five miles per hour on a calm twenty-degree day is facing a windchill of minus twenty. Combine that constant chill with driving sleet, snow, or rain, and a weatherproof shell jacket ($80 and up) could be considered a survival item.

Socks are a critical component of any outdoor outfit, and even day hikers would do well to have a dry pair stashed in a pocket. In a survival situation you cannot be too kind to your feet because they are probably the vehicle that will take you home. Socks are also a layered system, with a lightweight, slippery liner sock of nonabsorbent material, covered by a thicker insulated outersock. Liner socks cost about $6 a pair at outfitter stores, but department store acrylic dress socks are cheaper and perform as well. Outersocks (I like the SmartWool brand) retail for about $10 per pair but give years of service. Once again cotton in any amount is bad; cotton socks can make feet feel cold in the best boots, while a good sock system gets the most warmth from an inadequate boot. Avoid the mistake of pulling on additional socks, as these can constrict circulation through the feet and actually make them cold.

Proper boots are critically important. In summer your preferred hiking boots are fine, but when air temperatures drop below forty degrees Fahrenheit your toes will get cold; if you should get stranded for several days in hiking boots while snowshoeing, for example, count on losing some toes at least. People who know winter put away the hikers in fall and get out the pac boots. Simply described, a pac boot is a rugged waterproof shell with a removable insulated bootie liner for arctic-rated models and internal liners for less-frigid snows. Internal-liner boots, like Columbia's Ice Field model, start at less than a hundred dollars, have a comfort rating of minus forty, and are generally the most lightweight and best suited for snow hiking. Full-blown pac boots offer the option of sleeping with liners only to help keep the feet warm, with comfort ratings below minus one hundred degrees and prices ranging from about $100 to more than $200.

Handwear is also critical because fingers are even more vulnerable to cold than toes. While mittens are supposed to be warmer than gloves, most people prefer to have their fingers free. Insulation like Thinsulate and Comfortemp encased in weatherproof shells makes gloves as warm as mittens, even in wet, windy conditions. In very cold weather I wear a light knit acrylic liner under the main glove—available from the children's section in department stores for less than $1 per pair. Superwarm snowmobiling gloves with gauntlet-length wrists retail for around $40 a pair.

A head cover is important; the indispensable hood on your parka shell can be a blessing in driving rain or snow but should be backed up by an inexpensive ski mask (about $5) made from acrylic yarn and permanently residing in a jacket pocket. In bitterly cold temperatures the ski mask can be worn pulled down, even under a helmet, to protect the frostbite-prone nose and cheekbones, or rolled up to cover just the ears and head. There are fancier hats, but a knit ski mask and windproof parka hood have proved comfortable in windchills of minus sixty degrees Fahrenheit.

Because the layers in cold weather clothing systems are removed and added as needed, a place to stash clothing is essential. Some off-road and snow machines have storage space to suffice, but a day pack survival kit (see pp. 60–61 in chapter 1) kept fastened to the machine under normal conditions is portable—should you have to hike—with room for dry socks and glove liners, munchies, and survival items.

Put all of these together and you have a survival shelter that can be worn, even while hiking. Inside this traveling shell of protection from nature's wrath, you remain warm, nearly dry, and not chilled by gale-force winds. In a pinch, you can even sleep in the rain, hood up, usually in a sitting position against a backrest; it ain't Best Western, but I've survived through it a few times.

With a full backpack-size survival outfit (about forty pounds, with three days of food), and a few survival skills, you can survive indefinitely in almost any environment.

Heating a Shelter

Most survival students ask about this. If you have a survival out-fit the size of a day pack or larger, you need neither shelter nor warmth from a fire because those needs are addressed by the gear carried in the pack. As campers who insist on trying to cook in them prove from time to time, tents will melt if exposed to fire so never try to heat one. The presumption is that anyone with the foresight to have a survival outfit that includes shelter and a bed-roll will also have equipped it with a sleeping bag and bivy that are up to snuff for the region being visited.

Many survival shelters, constructed wholly or partly from dead wood and brush, are also flammable. The key to heating a shelter of any design is to capture heat radiated by a fire and reflect it back toward the doorway. Almost any solid or semisolid barrier erected on the side of the fire opposite the shelter door will serve to bounce concentrated heat back toward the opening. Reflectors should be at least six feet from the fire, especially if they are flammable, and may by formed by tying a space blanket between two trees, build-ing a wall of snow, or just making a pile of brush. Where terrain permits, reflectors can be natural, from cliff faces to the massed root systems of wind-toppled trees.

The Lean-To

The lean-to is the most familiar outdoor shelter. Simple and quick to build in almost every type of terrain, it can be constructed without tools. The frame consists of a main crosspiece held horizontal and about four feet off the ground by a pole or suspended from crotches in two adjacent trees. The crosspiece will have to be strong enough to support the roof, so it should be made from a stout, dead sapling roughly four inches in diameter and at least six feet long. The ends of the crosspiece are fastened to the vertical uprights by notching the uprights and tying the crosspiece in place with cord, or the forks of existing branches can be used to support the crosspiece.

The fastened crosspiece should be capable of supporting the survivalist's entire body weight without coming loose at either end. Accumulated snow can add more than a hundred pounds of weight to the roof and a windstorm can break large dead branches loose from overhead. Having the roof fall in or a large branch come crashing through—or just worrying about those things—can ruin a good night's sleep.

With the crosspiece in place, lay a sloping roof of long dead saplings and branches placed parallel to one another and extending from the cross-support to the ground. The ends that rest on the ground should be kept as even with one another as possible, regardless of how far the opposite ends stick out beyond the crosspiece. In fact, those saplings that do not stick out from the crosspiece will provide a convenient place to hang wet clothing, firearms, and other assorted gear. When the roof of saplings and branches is covered with a frame of dead wood it will not be watertight, but it will be solid enough to hold a layer of more dense vegetation.

When all the roof poles are in place over the crosspiece, the shelter will be strong but not waterproof or windproof. The easiest method of weatherproofing the roof is to cover it with a space blanket, poncho, or plastic drop cloth, held in place by the weight of more poles, sticks, and branches. In winter the roof can be sealed with a layer of packed snow. In a hardwood forest there is always a thick layer of flattened, decaying leaves that can be peeled from

THE LEAN-TO

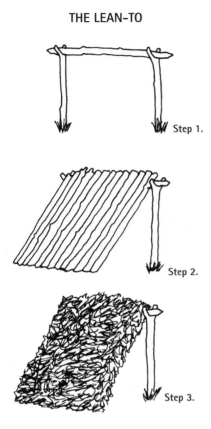

Step 1.

Step 2.

Step 3.

the ground in sections and placed like shingles over the roof poles, beginning at the lowest end and overlapping the rows from above so that water will run down the slope of the roof without leaking inside.

For long-term use—a plane crash on the wrong side of a mountain range at the start of winter, for example—more permanent roofing materials may be used. Dead logs and stumps rot from the inside out, leaving solid shells that can be broken off in curved sections (something like clay Spanish tiles) and laid onto the roof shingle fashion. Tough birch bark can be stripped away in sheets by driving your knife tip through the bark of fallen logs into the rotting interior and carefully drawing the cutting edge along its length to the log's end, then peeling it off in large pieces.

Although essentially a warm weather shelter because of its airy open front and sides, the lean-to can be modified into an excellent long-term shelter by adding another sloping roof on the open side of the crosspiece, over what had been the front. The result is a chalet-style shelter with a peaked roof. Another leaning wall against one of the open ends turns the shelter into a virtual cave, and shrinking the opening at the opposite end in the same manner leaves a doorway that can be heated by a small reflected

Bracken ferns are a plentiful summer roof covering across the U.S., but wear leather cloves, and cut them off at the stems—don't pull them out because razor-sharp stem fibers can slice bare skin like a knife.

fire. Despite its simplicity, the lean-to turned A-frame is very good shelter for long-term survival, with lots of interior space and good heat retention that can be enhanced just by piling more layers of forest debris atop the outer walls.

The Versatile Debris Shelter

The debris shelter is a usually compact long- or short-term emergency den that is constructed from whatever the surrounding terrain provides. The name alludes to a specific type of shelter, but no two debris shelters are exactly alike, and construction materials can vary broadly, from high-desert sagebrush to alpine evergreens to northern swamp moss. The beauty of a debris shelter is that once you have a grasp of its basics it can be constructed in virtually any terrain—even snowbound forest—so a creative eye is beneficial when scouting for building materials.

The most important component for all debris-type shelters is a main support, a stout pole eight to ten feet long, three or more inches in diameter at the base. Suitable candidates can often be found standing upright but dead, because some trees do not live to maturity. Ideal choices will stand more than a dozen feet tall and are dry enough to snap off when you push hard against them but are solid and nonrotted throughout. Bridge the thinnest end of the pole across a solid object, and heel-stomp or chop it to length; a suitably long main support should be at least two inches in diameter at its narrow end.

Elevate the thick end of the main support by wedging it into the limb crotch of a standing tree, into a rock crack, or onto an X frame of two saplings that have been lashed together and crossed—whatever solid support will hold it at least three feet above the ground. It is important for the narrow end of the pole to be the one against the earth, because if it should give under the weight of snow, for example, only a few inches at the low end will likely break, and the entire shelter will not come crashing down. At this point, install the sleeping pallet on the ground directly below and parallel to the main support. This critical part of any emergency shelter serves to keep a sleeper's body from making direct contact with the earth, which will absorb body heat faster than the body can generate it, even in summer. In woodlands, the usual configuration is a platform formed by placing relatively straight, body-length, dead saplings and limbs on the ground alongside one another until a rough bed, about two feet wide, takes shape. The minimum diameter of each pallet member should be two inches to ensure adequate insulation.

The shelter's triangular walls are constructed by leaning lengths of branches at an angle between the main support and the ground from either side. The amount of floor space is determined by how far apart the wall supports are set, but a smaller interior space retains body heat better. Place a few "framing" sticks against the main support to set the shelter's internal dimensions, then add on to that skeleton with more layers of dead sticks. Set the placement and size of the triangle-shaped door at the high end on the shelter's leeward side, faced away from prevailing winds (some prefer to set it at the open, highest end, but this forces feetfirst entry). Although the shelter is held in place only by friction and weight, every wall stick added increases overall strength. Note that shorter sticks can be used at the lower foot end of the shelter, and it doesn't matter if a wall stick extends beyond the main support—in fact, having wall sticks cross in an X above the main support provides a place to hang wet clothing and frequently needed gear. Add branches to the wall, including the head end, until only the inverted V doorway is left uncovered and gaps of less than two inches exist between the sticks.

The next step is to seal the frame to keep air inside the shelter as motionless as possible, impervious to howling winds outside and able to shrug off rainstorms of less than biblical proportions. In many places bracken ferns are an ideal roof covering until winter snows bury them, but so are layers of wet, compressed leaves peeled

The skeletal frame of a debris shelter (note that sleeping pallet is already in place below) can be sealed against the elements with whatever is available—including packed snow.

from the forest floor or clumps of sphagnum moss pulled from the ground in a cedar swamp. The objective is to seal the shelter frame sufficiently to block out daylight—and rain—and almost any material that will cover an area of the frame is suitable. Remember to shingle the roof beginning at the bottom with a row of overlapping cover material, with each ascending row overlapping the one below, to ensure that rain runs off.

Alternatively, a quicker, slightly more skeletal frame can be erected and simply draped with a tarp or a painter's plastic drop cloth. In winter, the frame can be sealed with packed snow to form a solid shell that retains body heat more efficiently than a double-wall tent. Whatever roofing material you use, add another layer of spaced-apart poles over it to hold everything in place should a wind come up.

While not quite a night at Best Western, it'll help keep you warm and dry for as long as you need.

When no daylight penetrates the roof, add a thick layer of dry foliage–dead leaves, ferns, grass–to the sleeping pallet inside to soften protuberances and add insulation. Dry foliage can also serve as a blanket, trapping radiated body heat with surprising effectiveness. In a pinch, green foliage will suffice better than no padding, but the moisture in green vegetation means that it is constantly cooling as it dries, and some–like pine boughs–exude gluelike sap for days after being cut. The goal is to create an effective shield between your body and the cooling effects of earth and air. Whatever material you use to accomplish that, a good rule of thumb is to use more than you think you'll need.

As mentioned doorways should always be placed away from prevailing winds, but preferably the shelter site will itself be isolated from wind. The doorway can be closed to minimize heat-stealing air flow by pulling a layer of dead branches over it from the inside or covering it with a ground sheet, slabs of wood pulled from the outer shells of rotting stumps, or sheets of birch bark stripped from fallen trees.

Or you might opt to leave the doorway uncovered with a small fire outside about five feet in front of the opening, far enough to avoid burning the combustible (never forget that) shelter but close enough to radiate warmth to its interior. A reflector wall of dead wood, snow, or anything else that can be stacked densely to a height of at least two feet helps to bounce radiated heat back toward the shelter opening and block ground winds.

In most environments, a single-occupant debris hut can be built solo, and with no tools, in well under three hours. Despite its ease of construction some debris shelters have withstood heavy winter snows for more than ten years; the design is functional anywhere it can be built, and a few have literally served as home to adventurers for months at a time. Subzero windchills and wind-driven precipitation have no effect inside its walls, and solid construction promotes a greater sense of security than collapsible fabric shelters. If you had to, you could live in, and build on to, this shelter for years.

The Dugout

A cross between a military bunker and the sod houses of early prairie farmers (sometimes called sodbusters) who had no other building materials, an earthen dugout is the most permanent of survival shelters. It is also the most laborious to build, so it is definitely for long-term survival. The payoff is that a dugout allows you to weather any storm, from blizzards to hurricanes, in relative comfort. If the survivalist (we'll assume a plane-crash survivor) has a folding entrenching tool, the job can be accomplished more easily. Lacking a shovel, the dugout can be excavated with a slab of wood and bare hands, but it might take a day to do it and burn a couple thousand calories.

The first step in dugout construction is to select a location. Low hills are a good choice as long as they're located on high ground where rain runoff or melting spring snow won't flood the shelter. The peaks of larger, especially bald, hills from which a signal fire or stretched-out reflective space blanket can be seen are good candidates. When possible, save labor by incorporating natural terrain features, like large splits in a rock face, into the design.

EARTH DUGOUT

Long-Term Extreme Cold Weather Shelter
(Shown in Cross Section)

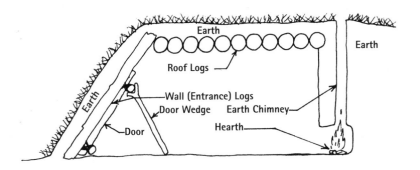

Once a site has been selected, the work begins. In lieu of a proper entrenching tool, a sturdy slab of wood can be used to dig away the soil after loosening it, along with a knife to hack through roots. The finished excavation may be as large as the builder wishes, but four feet deep by seven feet long by seven feet wide is livable and a good compromise between labor invested and benefit acquired. Keep all excavated soil in a pile nearby because it will be used later to cover the roof.

When finished, the excavation should look like a square hole cut into the side of a hill with the top open. Make the roof by laying several large, dead logs across the hole with as little gap between each one as possible until they cover the entire top of the excavation. Remaining gaps are covered with wet leaves, ferns, or anything else that can be stuffed into them. The builder should periodically crawl inside to check for open spots that might be missed when seen from above. When all the cracks have been stopped up, the roof is recovered with the soil that was removed during excavation. Sod should be used first because its dense clusters of grass roots will act as a screen to prevent looser soil from shaking down through the roof beams. When all the sod has been laid back over the log roof, the remainder of the soil is simply piled on top of it. The finished roof will be thick, well insulated, and waterproof in even the fiercest rainstorm.

But the front side of the dugout is still open; the easiest way to cover the front of the shelter is to lean more logs and large branches against the outside at an angle, placing them side by side with as little gap between each one as possible, forming a sloping wall that will provide a bit more room inside, while the incline provides a runoff for rain.

The center of the front wall must be left open to form the doorway, which should be kept as small as possible. When the walls on either side of the doorway are finished and the entrance is the desired size, plug the gaps between logs and cover them as thoroughly as possible with dirt. Again, sod should be placed over the logs first and loose soil piled on top of that.

The door is a separate unit that opens from the inside. A door that opens outward is always a bad idea in snow country, where a storm might dump several feet of heavy, wet snow overnight, making it impossible to open the door. If you have a supply of parachute cord or nylon string, a door frame can be lashed together, with foliage tied in place to cover it. You can make the door by lashing a row of large, straight branches to a horizontal crosspiece at either end. If cordage is unavailable, the door can be constructed by weaving a heavy mat of green branches together, but a woven door is more work to build. The most expedient method is to use slabs split from the solid outer shells of rotting logs or stumps. When the completed door has been taken inside the shelter, a stout branch about two feet long with a Y-shaped crotch at one end can be used to hold the door in place from inside; wedge the Y under the top crosspiece and lightly kick the bottom of the brace toward the door until it fits snugly in place.

Unlike other shelters, which are heated by fires placed near the entrance, the dugout contains its own fireplace for heating and cooking in bad weather. The fireplace should be located against the back wall and situated so that sparks and hot coals that pop out of it during use won't damage the occupant's bed or equipment. When a suitable location has been determined, begin by digging a squared hole into the wall approximately two feet in width by two feet long by two feet deep. The bottom of the fireplace should be at least six inches below the floor of the shelter to prevent hot coals from overflowing in the living space. Excess coals and ashes can be removed later with a flat slab of wood and spread outside the shelter entrance over the snow to keep it from becoming slippery and dangerous to walk on.

The next step is to punch out a chimney from the fireplace to the surface. This is best accomplished from the inside by using a knife to gouge a hole upward. Be sure to leave a minimum of one foot of insulating soil between the chimney hole and the inside wall of the shelter. Keep the inside diameter of the chimney as small as possible at first and widen it to a consistent six to eight inches afterward by ramming a log of about the same size through it. Using a branch to widen the hole will ensure that the inside wall of the chimney is smooth and straight and will conduct smoke outside as efficiently as possible.

Even with a dinner-plate-size fire, the little dugout fireplace is a very efficient heater, largely because of the high insulation properties of earth. Laying a small fire before turning in at night will heat a sealed dugout until dawn on all but the coldest of nights. In fact, the occupant may wake up overheated and perspiring before getting a feel for how much wood to use. Smoke should not be a problem except in high winds that produce a downdraft in the chimney. The amount of smoke produced can be kept to a minimum by using only dry hotter-burning wood. If the chimney does develop a downdraft, the problem can usually be remedied by cracking the door open a few inches. If the fireplace fills the living space with smoke no matter what you try, the chimney needs to be widened—not too much, though, because the wider the flue, the more heat it will carry outside.

The Snow Dugout

The snow dugout is an expedient emergency shelter during a winter storm that dumps several feet of snow on the ground. A more comfortable variation on the basic snow trench, it offers a bit more protection for a lot less work. I credit this shelter with saving my life in February of 1984 when a not unusual northern Michigan blizzard dumped six feet of drifted snow on the countryside, causing snow plows to be grounded for the duration and stranding me for three days. In that instance the temperature dropped forty degrees in an afternoon, and windchills on the flats—according to my pocket radio—were gusting to minus forty. Even in the windbreak of a mature hardwood forest, I needed a shelter quickly to escape that killing wind. Thanks to the snow dugout, I spent the next three days in relative comfort until the weather allowed me to leave.

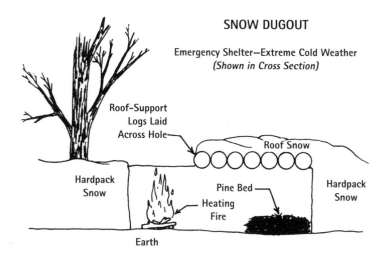

SNOW DUGOUT

Emergency Shelter—Extreme Cold Weather
(Shown in Cross Section)

Roof-Support
Logs Laid
Across Hole

Roof Snow

Hardpack
Snow

Pine Bed

Heating
Fire

Hardpack
Snow

Earth

Building a snow dugout requires at least four feet of hardpack snow on the ground, because the depth of the snow determines the height of the shelter's ceiling. The upside is that with deep snows covering most of the usual wood and vegetation that could be used for construction, this shelter makes good use of what is at hand: snow.

The beauty of the snow dugout lies not only in its effectiveness but in the speed with which it can be built. The first step is to lay a wood platform of heavy sticks side by side atop the snow. Then build a big fire on top of this platform. Like woodsmen of old I normally prefer small fires for cooking and heating, but in this case a survivalist should literally pour on the wood to create as large a blaze as can be managed—there is little danger of starting a forest fire on hardpack snow and the fire might be noticed by anyone searching for you or who happens to be in the area. As the fire gains strength it will begin to melt through the snow. Keep piling on the wood. Before long the fire will have melted the snow down to the ground. At this point the fire's heat will be focused against the snow walls surrounding it and the hole will melt outward, increasing in diameter as a growing patch of bare ground becomes exposed. When the hole in the hardpack has grown to a diameter of seven feet, let the fire die down, and reduce it to a smaller fire at one edge of the hole. The smaller heating and cooking fire should be located directly across from where you intend to sleep to help maximize the heat radiated toward you.

Next comes the roof made from dead logs and saplings that are longer than the width of the melted hole and collected by simply pushing over dead standing tree trunks (especially barkless pines and aspen) that stick out of the snow. Lay a platform of wood pieces placed side by side, ends supported atop the snow, across the top of the hole. Viewed from above, the parallel roof should cover half the hole opening—the roof should provide enough cover to keep your body protected from falling rain or snow while you sleep. When the roof beams are all in place, seal gaps between them with smaller sticks, slabs of bark, even chunks of rotting log. The objective is to provide a solid, insulated base to support the thick layer of packed snow that will finish and seal the roof.

All that remains is to lay a generous bed of springy green pine boughs on the ground under the protective roof to keep the sleeper's body heat from being absorbed into the frozen ground. Remember, direct body contact with the ground is the surest way to get a dose of hypothermia even with a fire, so the more padded the makeshift sleeping pallet the better. If you have room to crawl in between the bed and the roof, the bed is not too thick.

Emergency Shelters

Like any traveler, a survivor trying to get back to civilization needs a place to sleep a few rejuvenating hours each day. The best sleeping times will not always be during the hours of darkness because days are warmer—or hotter—than nights, mosquitoes are fewer in sunlight, and blackflies bite only during daylight. No matter what hours work best for sleeping and trekking, you will probably need some type of shelter to help shield you from precipitation, sun, or bugs, and a typical survival shelter is just too much work for a single night's accommodations. If conditions allow, the simplest bed is under an open sky, but some type of shelter is always best.

Tripod Shelter

If you have a space blanket, tarp, or poncho, the tripod shelter is an expedient tent that can be created from almost any environment. The four required components are three relatively straight poles, each at least an inch in diameter at its narrowest point, and about a foot of cord. Cut two of the poles to a length of three feet; the remaining pole should be at least eight feet long. Lay the three poles on the ground so that their ends are even, placing the longest pole between the shorter poles, and loosely tie a single loop of cord around all three members, about six inches from their ends. Cross the two shorter poles under the longer pole to form an X. Place the longest pole in the crotch of that X and raise the center pole as you bring the shorter support poles up and forward to form an irregular tripod. As you do, you will note that the cord twists and becomes tight, so that the frame joint is solid and held in place as if it were lashed together.

A survivor's level of preparation increases with the distance he or she will be from outside help; in the far back country, the survival kit should be capable of addressing almost every need, from building a primitive shelter to the latest in first-aid.

With the frame erect, add a sleeping pallet and a mattress of foliage. Finally, drape the frame with your waterproof covering, and crawl in out of the rain. Inside, you can make other adjustments, like tucking loose ends of the space blanket under the bottoms of the support poles to hold against the wind. In the morning, just remove and pocket the covering and cord, and be on your way.

Natural Shelters

If you need shelter, try looking at your surroundings with a creative eye. The forces of nature often do all or part of the job for you. A tree trunk that has snapped in the wind four feet above ground but still very solidly attached to its stump is a ready-made main support for a debris shelter. A toppled tree whose trunk is suspended above ground by its root system can do the same, and in some cases you can simply hack out a living space from attached branches on the underside of the trunk.

Stream banks that were undercut during high water can be good overnight shelters. In rock country, these undercuts are likely to be ageless shallow caves that once sheltered traveling bands of skin-clad hunters armed with spears. In a forest, stream banks are likely to be overhung by massed roots and dirt that would be perilous to step onto from above, so be choosy about where you sleep.

Opinions vary, but for me, deep caves are not a preferred place to camp. Winds can fill them with smoke that lingers for a long time; in winter the rock stays cold, like a refrigerator; and caves are sometimes within the claimed domain of other species, especially in foul weather. Shallow rock undercuts, large cracks in a cliff face, even chimneys, may be preferable to camping in a cold cavern. Wherever you camp in rock country, always be mindful that water is not absorbed, and a quarter inch of rain falling on high land can become a raging whitewater torrent by the time it reaches sea level; avoid gullies, always try to camp on elevated ground, and beware of places where fine sand or vegetation has been massed by currents.

Before selecting any shelter site, step back and observe it with a critical eye. The snow-weighted branches of a large hemlock can look like a ready-made shelter, but large clumps of snow in the upper branches are guaranteed to come tumbling down unpleasantly on whatever is below. Avoid making camp within a hundred yards of established animal trails—especially in bear country, and especially during the June/July mating season. Always look upward when selecting a campsite in the forest, keeping away from dead standing trees that might break and fall over in a wind; they are called *widow makers* in logging country.

As with every aspect of practical survival, ingenuity and imagination are integral to finding, adapting, or creating a warm and secure place to sleep, or even live indefinitely. The survival-oriented eye doesn't see rocks, trees, and mud in a wilderness, but building materials and tools for making life easier.

THREE

Fire

The importance of fire in any survival situation cannot be overstated. Had survivors of Hurricane Katrina made a small fire and had a metal gas can, three feet of garden hose, and basic survival skills, they could have distilled the most polluted water in quantity. Thirsty victims (many of whom would not drink their own tap water prior to that) would not have been forced to drink from putrid waters. Boiling alone doesn't remove harmful chemicals, but it does kill all organisms in water and food. Cooking foods, either plants or meat, breaks down tough proteins and makes them more digestible, and most people prefer cooked foods to raw.

Fire also gives a survivor the means to alert distant rescuers with smoke and light, and it virtually guarantees that no one will suffer from the cold. Its heat warms the soul as well as the body, making any dilemma a little less dismal; fires have been a source of ideas since mankind discovered their powers.

None of those vital uses for fire has the life-saving urgency of making a fire to stave off or remedy hypothermia. An ice fisherman who has just been dragged out of a hole in thin ice doesn't have enough lifetime left to warm up the car or maybe even wait for an ambulance to arrive. There are a multitude of serious reasons for needing the emergency warmth of a fire, and you can almost bet that all of them will occur in an environment that is not conducive to making a fire—in fact, that seems to be a rule. Troubles are amplified if you're alone, numb fingers curling involuntarily into lifeless claws, abdominal muscles cramping as they try to keep vital organs warm, and miserable spasms of uncontrollable shivering that make simple tasks undoable. There is no time to waste with fire-making tools that cannot produce immediate results.

Tinder

Tinder is the first, most critical, component of making a fire. The most common mistake made by beginners is trying to light a campfire by applying flame to wood that is too massive to be lighted. Every fire begins small, starting with easily flammable tinder materials that burn hot and fast in open air. The burn duration of tinder materials is typically short, but the idea is to use a brief, hot flame to ignite slightly larger dry twigs, then branches, until a hot bed of red coals below provides enough heat to burn the largest pieces of wood.

I don't believe there is any terrain where vegetation grows that doesn't provide tinder for making a fire. Tinders that catch fire with a hot spark or flame include dried reindeer moss (not really a moss

While it has tasted awful in every recipe ever tried, Reindeer Moss is a near-perfect survival food—after it has been boiled to remove its laxative properties—that is found in "barren" places on every continent.

but a lichen), dead grasses, fine strips of birch bark, or the massed fibers of sections of dead aspen or poplar bark, separated by crumbling the brittle bark from around them. Pine needles shed from the tree contain resins that make them burn easily, and even damp ones that won't keep burning can be coaxed by gently blowing on the coals. The same is true of tiny, dry pine twigs found at the end of dead pine branches; one of my survival class demonstrations is to hold a small bundle of tiny dead pine twigs in one hand and light them into a flaming mass using only a butane lighter. Even in the dead of winter, grass stems sticking above the snow reveal that there are more freeze-dried and flammable grasses below.

Dried tree sap, or pitch, exuded from woodpecker holes and other injuries in pine, cherry, and some other trees is always flammable once it has been heated to a liquid state and is long burning enough to have once been used for torches made of pitch-saturated grass. A lump of pitch melted onto small twigs with a match is usually enough to set them afire.

If no suitable natural tinder is available, you can make your own by reducing larger pieces of dry wood to more flammable shavings and splinters. The process is as simple as whittling off a small mound of shavings from available dry wood with your knife (a sharpened rock won't do here). The smaller and finer the shavings, the more easily they will ignite, but count on needing a plate-size mound of shavings to create a flame of sufficient duration to ignite larger twigs.

The best and most fail-safe tinder materials should always come from your own pocket. The simplest, cheapest, and all-around best of manufactured survival tinders is the Fire Wick, which is essentially nothing more than cotton laundry/packaging string that has been dipped into molten paraffin (canning wax), cooled until stiff, then cut into sections and packaged for carry. Some survivalists get fancy by twist-locking or braiding string into thick lengths before dipping to create heavy, long-burning wicks. Some get the same effect from doubling a string several times and tying the combined string into large knots before dipping it in wax. Wool felt weather stripping, available in rolls from hardware stores, is a good alternative; it absorbs more wax and burns longer but is harder to light. With either material, one end or corner of the tinder should be frayed with a fingernail prior to lighting.

Other home-brewed tinders include cotton balls saturated with petroleum jelly and carried in a pill bottle (too messy for me), cardboard or cotton flannel saturated with paraffin, or scraps of singed cotton flannel (char cloth) carried in a watertight tinder box. If you have a gun, the bullet can be levered from a cartridge and the powder inside can be used to ignite tinder. In a pinch, a bulletless

When starting a fire, avoid the common mistake of smothering burning tinder with wood that is too heavy to ignite; note the handful of tiny dry twigs this survivalist is adding one at a time, carefully building the fire hot enough to eventually consume logs.

cartridge with the powder still inside can be plugged with a ball of dried grasses (only at the cartridge end) and discharged with the muzzle inside a mass of easily lighted tinder. Although very cool when it works, the muzzle blast sometimes just throws tinder aside without lighting it and you waste precious ammo with every attempt, so use this method judiciously.

Military fuel bars, like the trioxane and hexamine used by the American and British armies, usually are sold inexpensively in Army/Navy surplus stores and catalogs, and either is a must-have for an all-weather fire-starting kit. Made for cooking with a small folding stove, these fuel bars ignite at the touch of a flame in any weather, and burn hot for several minutes.

Preparing a Fire Pit

The first step in starting a campfire is to find a suitable location. When using a shelter, the fire should always be located directly in front of the entrance but at a distance that will keep flames or sparks from setting the shelter afire. In windy weather the fire and shelter should be located on the lee side of a hill or in thickly wooded terrain to help block air currents that can blow hot sparks into the woods and create a windchill factor in the shelter in cold weather. As an added precaution, all combustible debris should be scraped or kicked away from the campfire for at least three feet in all directions.

The next step is to create a fire pit to help contain popping coals, block wind, and to reflect radiated heat onto the coal bed, making the fire bed hotter. The traditional method of creating a fire pit is to place large stones around its circumference; stones absorb and hold heat from the fire up to many hours, and a cold survivalist can use heated stones to keep warm through the night by placing one at the foot of a bedroll or even just hugging a large one against the belly. Be warned never to expose stones taken from a stream bed to fire; it rarely happens, but I've seen waterlogged stones heat and explode like a grenade. In lieu of stones, excavate the fire pit to a diameter of about eighteen inches by six inches deep and arrange the excavated soil into a low fire wall surrounding the pit's perimeter.

Starting a Fire

The next step is to lay the fire in preparation for lighting; begin by placing the tinder material—which can be a mixture of different tinders—in the center of the fire pit. A platform of finger-thick dead sticks laid parallel on the ground beneath the tinder, and especially atop snow, gives your fledgling fire a head start, allowing it to develop a hot coal bed before making contact with wet earth. Once a good coal bed has been established, a fire—insulated from below by its own ashes—will just melt away the snow around it until it reaches bare ground, but a platform is essential to efficient fire making. Lay your tinder in a loose, airy mass in the center of the platform.

Next, build a tepee of small dry sticks, none bigger than a pencil, all around the circumference of the tinder pile so that they come together and support one another about eight inches above the floor of the fire pit. This cone-shaped picket of kindling helps to keep the tinder from blowing away and provides an umbrella for the tinder fire, while allowing maximum exposure of each stick to the flames. The tepee method of arranging kindling will ensure that a sizable air gap exists between the tinder pile and the sticks above it, as well as between the kindling sticks themselves.

When the woods are wet, you might use a manufactured tinder (Fire Wicks, trioxane, hexamine) for the initial stage, using it to dry then ignite waterlogged natural tinders, which in turn burn long and hot enough to dry and ignite the kindling tepee. When the woods are wet, take kindling sticks for the tepee from the trunks of standing trees, some of which will always have dead twigs attached within easy reach. Shielded from rain by foliage and suspended in open air, dead twigs still attached to trunks are always the driest, whereas those lying on the ground are likely to remain damp for

STARTING A FIRE WITH WET WOOD, TEPEE METHOD

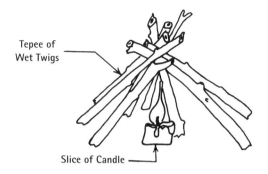

Tepee of
Wet Twigs

Slice of Candle

weeks. Wood from the ground is fine for a campfire that has a self-sustaining bed of coals—in fact, wet rotting wood thrown on hot coals is good for making signals and as an insect repellent—but starting a fire requires the driest kindling you can find.

With the platform, tinder, and kindling tepee in place, apply a flame to the tinder, either directly using a match or lighter or with a lighted fire wick or other combustible material. A good flint and steel, like the Strike Force, permits the grip and pressure

Blowing on the coals
to bolster a fire.

needed to strike sparks hot enough to ignite even damp tinders. Add more tinder to the base of the tepee until the tepee sticks begin to flame hotly, then carefully add more sticks one at a time to avoid smothering the still-weak flames. When a solid bed of red coals has formed on the platform, begin laying progressively larger kindling sticks lengthwise and parallel to one another on top of the coals. Gently blow into the coals until they glow hotly, causing the fresh sticks to smoke then flame. Continue adding more wood until the parallel stack is as large as you need it to be.

Getting Firewood

Where you can start a fire, there will probably be fuel to sustain it, but the available large-diameter, long-burning logs will not be in convenient lengths. Do not waste energy trying to break large wood to fire-size lengths; the simplest method is to simply lay the ends of two or more large trunks onto the coal bed from opposite sides, parallel to one another. As the ends are consumed, feed each length farther into the fire. Alternatively, you can burn lengths in half, but if the length is elevated at either end, be prepared for the fire to burn down under and away from the log; you might have to keep adding wood from below before large ones burn in half.

Trees are constantly shedding dead branches—sometimes live ones in heavy snowfalls—and there should be an abundance of smaller branches on the ground, along with a few wind-sheared treetops and an occasional whole dead tree. Drag lengths to your fire, butt end first, as the natural upward angle of still-attached branches helps to keep them from snagging against other trees. On deep hardpack snow, all firewood must come from standing trees, and sometimes standing dead trees will have rotted enough to be pushed over and dragged back to your fire.

Be sure to lay in a good supply of wood before making camp each night because even if you have a flashlight, there is a potential for injury in untracked woods. You could walk off a cliff or turn an ankle or get poked by a twig in the eyeball.

Gathering firewood in minus–fifteen–degree weather.

The Heating Fire

Every fire generates heat, but how a fire is arranged can determine how efficient it is as a body heater. Many cold nights have proved that placing firewood lengths side by side atop the coals works best. Seen from the ends, wood stacked in this fashion resembles a pyramid, and, like a pyramid, this "furnace pile" can be built higher by adding more wood. Built onto an already hot fire, a furnace pile uses large-diameter pieces of wood to maximize burning time, and permits using wood of all lengths and diameters. This type of heating fire is directional, throwing most of its heat to either long side of the stack, but its energy should always be channeled through the use of a reflector.

The Hot Bed

The hot bed is an old invention by mountain men to help keep them warm during cold winter nights in the open when a five-point wool horse blanket was the standard bedroll. Anyone who has ever slept in the open air on even a warm summer night can attest to the amount of body heat lost. The hot bed helped to counteract this by providing a constant, if steadily diminishing, source of heat from below. Properly constructed, it will keep a person warm throughout the night, even in very cold weather.

The hot bed can best be prepared with the help of a small shovel or entrenching tool, but even a slab of wood will work in most instances. The first step is to build a long, hot fire that measures about four feet wide by seven feet in length. The fire should be fueled until a solid bed of red coals is formed and allowed to burn down. The glowing bed of coals is then covered with a layer of loose dirt or sand at least four inches thick and tamped down as much as possible. An alternate method is to excavate a shallow, body-length depression and then shovel the hot coals into it, covering them with the dirt taken from the excavation. Both methods are equally effective, but the first one requires a bit less effort.

The dirt-covered hot bed is well insulated and can be used without further work, but my own experience has been that the normal rolling and shifting of position that occurs during sleep is apt to scrape away the protective earth and expose the sleeper to a rude, painful awakening. As protection against this I recommend laying a thin layer of pine boughs or leafy branches over the dirt. A poncho thrown over the dirt will also work to keep the dirt in place, but keep in mind that doing so also exposes the poncho to the possibility of being burned.

The Cooking Fire

Cooking over an open fire requires a bit more skill than one might think. The most common error made by campers is trying to cook over a flaming campfire; a campfire produces far more heat than an electric or gas range, and food cooked over its flames will likely char on the outside before it can be cooked on the inside.

A fire made using the furnace pile configuration of parallel logs usually provides at least one flat, heated spot to set a cooking vessel on. Flames forced from below through gaps between burning logs make ideal range burners. The larger logs do not burn away from below a cook pot causing it to spill over, and the steady focused heat blasting up from between them is easier to cook over. Bear in mind that when you cook over fire, you can't regulate the heat, so you regulate the exposure of the food being cooked—if the food is cooking too fast, move it farther from the heat.

The spit is a traditional way of cooking small animals over fire. This method doesn't require the use of any cooking utensils and is the easiest method of preparing wild game in a survival situation. The spit begins with two forked sticks set vertically into the ground on either side of the fire pit. The straight bottom end of each stick should be pushed at least six inches into the soil, and both should be stable enough not to fall over under the weight of the loaded spit. The crotch of these support sticks should be about two feet above the floor of the fire pit. The sticks should be made from green wood, although dry wood can be used as long as the sticks are placed far enough from the fire to keep them from burning.

The spit itself should always be constructed of green wood at least an inch in diameter and long enough to extend a minimum of four inches beyond the crotch of either support stick. The spit is sharpened on one end and threaded through the animal's rib cage, and on small mammals, through the pelvis. Small birds or fish are simply speared through the ribs and slid over the spit. Larger fish are spitted by piercing them at an angle near the tail, bending the body into a U, and piercing again near the head. When selecting wood for a spit, avoid using green pine or cedar. These resinous softwoods can impart a turpentine taste to cooked foods. Pine burns hot and fast, which is ideal for starting a fire or heating water in a container, but green conifer wood should not be used for cooking or smoking meat.

Suspend a spitted animal or fish over a low fire by setting the ends of the spit into the crotch of the support sticks and sliding the meat to the center of the spit. The fire beneath the spit should

A squirrel carcass, spitted and ready for roasting.

always be kept as low as possible and the meat should be turned frequently. Cook all wild meat or fish thoroughly—never eat raw wild game or fish, because most species can carry parasitic organisms that can infect humans. The addition of green birch, aspen, or maple will cause the fire to smoke and help sweeten the meat as it cooks.

Wilderness cooking is one of the activities in which the leather work gloves mentioned in chapter 1 will prove very useful. Fabric gloves should never be used as protection from heat, but leather gloves offer good protection when handling hot cookware or arranging burning wood. They aren't impervious to fire and common sense should be exercised to prevent burns, but they do allow a campfire cook to reach into the fire pit and quickly remove a canteen cup filled with boiling water without injury.

When boiling wild plants to eat, add about a tablespoon of wood ashes per quart of water. The practice of adding wood ashes to soups is a tradition among Indians and was long thought to be some type of ceremonial habit. In 1996 it was learned that caustic elements in wood ashes cause tough plant cellulose to break down, allowing the comparatively anemic human digestive system to convert otherwise indigestible proteins into usable amino acids. An ability to enhance the digestibility of tough plants (and meat) broadens your food choices, and helps you get the most from those you eat.

Placing large-diameter dead wood parallel onto a coal bed—a configuration known as the "furnace pile"—generates maximum heat, directed especially through gaps between logs, and provides level, stable cooking surfaces for your pots.

Banking a Fire

Aboriginal humans never extinguished their campfires unless they were leaving for a long time. In real life, putting out the fire to go hunting for a day was impractical, and maybe unwise, because it would be needed that evening, and conditions might not be so agreeable for making a fire then. The trick was to "bank" the fire so that it neither burned nor died out but remained at a smoldering idle that could be quickly rebuilt into a warm blaze. This uncomplicated, but seldom described, technique is basically little more than half smothering a bed of hot coals with one or more large-diameter logs placed on top of them, side by side if two or more are used. Good banking logs include wet rotting trunks that are too big and damp to catch fire, but can slowly dry and smolder just enough to keep the coals below hot. Just roll the logs over to expose hot coals that can be used to ignite tinder by gently blow-

Banked using nothing more than the charred end of a large dead log, this fire was banked to a smolder overnight, and easily rekindled the next, very cold, morning.

ing them to flaming hotness—when restarting a fire from coals, remember that dead coals placed atop red coals will reheat to red hot from contact. Left for too long, the banking logs will smolder away from the coal bed until the gap between them is too great and the coals starve.

The Signal Fire

Bob Garner, who once hosted *Michigan Out-of-Doors*, a public television program in Michigan, told me that his idea of wilderness survival was to "build a great big goddam fire and wait for someone to come and get me."

A signal fire differs from a cooking or heating fire by its large size and high visibility. It has to be large and bright to attract as much attention as possible from as many miles away as possible. The heat and sparks generated by such a big fire precludes it from being located anywhere near a shelter or other flammables. Bluffs, open beaches, and other clear, and preferably high, places are among the most visible choices for siting a signal fire.

To be as effective as possible, a signal fire must be as large as it can safely be, and it will consume a great deal of wood quickly. For that reason, the tall tepee-shaped pyre is probably best preassembled and left ready to be lighted from a smaller fire nearby. Construction of the ready-made signal fire begins with a hot-burning tinder, such as dried grass, topped by a large tepee of dried twigs and sticks from a fast-burning softwood. Next comes a larger tepee of heavier branches about six feet in length. The two tepees will help keep the tinder dry by forming a roof over it. Spotting a plane or some other potential rescuer, the survivalist lights the tinder, which lights the smaller tepee of sticks. The flames from the smaller tepee will in turn ignite the larger tepee, sending a brilliant pyre of flame into the sky to a height of ten feet or more.

Assuming that both tinder and wood are dry, the signal fire will flame up very quickly, usually within minutes. But be warned: the larger tepee will consume itself from the bottom up and can be expected to burn for no more than fifteen minutes before collapsing to one side. For this reason the signal fire must be located in a place where there's no danger of causing a forest fire when it falls over.

During the hours of darkness a signal fire can be seen for miles, but in daylight the flames fade to near obscurity. Watchers who man fire towers know that flames from even the hottest forest fire are difficult to see in full daylight, but a plume of smoke against the sky is highly visible. Armed with this knowledge, one can continue to signal during the day by building a large, hot fire and then partially smothering it with a layer of damp rotting wood or wet leaves. The coals will have enough heat to burn the damp material but not enough to ignite it, and the fire will smoke heavily.

FOUR
Water

In 2006 a client taking a survival course from a well-known outdoor survival school died of dehydration in a desert canyon just two hundred feet from a water hole. Toward the end, the victim was hallucinating, talking to cacti as if they were people. When the objective is to deliberately explore one's limits through extreme adversity (the hairy-man ideal), such a tragedy is almost inevitable at some point. There are just some things, such as thirst, cold, and heat, that no one can tough out, and when your life is on the line in a real situation, it would be stupid to try—you could die just practicing. Like the most powerful and rugged vehicle, our body requires fluids to remain at operational temperatures; take the fluids away from either machine and death is sure.

None of us can survive more than four or five days without water, even less if the weather is hot and exertion levels are high. Death by dehydration is neither fast nor pleasant, and even getting just enough water to get by is flirting with other complications of dehydration, such as severe constipation, a kidney infection, and other bugs that get a foothold while a body's defenses are compromised. In hot weather especially, the rule of thumb is to consume two gallons of water per day per person. Actual needs tend to be less, but it is important to never feel thirsty and to drink when you do.

Never attempt to conserve or ration water, not even if you're just practicing survival techniques. Many desert travelers have been found dead of dehydration with a half-full canteen on their side. The best place for your water is in your belly where it keeps the body—including your brain—running smoothly. Better to drink the water, then concentrate on ways of getting more.

Waterborne Diseases

The Food and Drug Administration estimates that about 370,000 Americans are afflicted with a waterborne parasite annually, and that about 80 percent of us have had one in the past. Feces are the source of most parasites, waterborne or otherwise, and although most animals do not defecate directly into their own drinking water, runoff from snow and rain ensures that the eggs (oocysts) of parasitic organisms will be washed into streams and lakes.

Science is still discovering all the animals that live in just a drop of pond water, but the three that campers and backpackers in North America should be most concerned with are *Giardia lamblia*, cryptosporidium, and cyclospora. These intestinal parasites remain infectious in every season and are not killed by freezing. The U.S. Fish and Wildlife Service has warned that nonaquatic tapeworms might be contracted from water sources on Lake Superior's Isle Royale National Park, their eggs probably washed in from infected wolf scats. Even so, we can count ourselves lucky not to have the heart, liver, and lung flukes (worms) common to tropical climes.

The scariest aspect of waterborne pathogens stems from our inability to see the microscopic creatures. Not every drink of water will contain parasites, but virtually every waterway will support a population of them somewhere. Flowing water is not free of parasites, regardless of how fast the current or how pristine the geography. The only natural water sources that are safe to drink from are springheads where subterranean water flows directly from the earth, and even then only at the source.

To add even more mystery, two hikers might drink from the same water hole and only one will become sick. This could be because one of them simply did not drink in any parasites, or one person's immune system was strong enough to overcome the invaders before they could get a foothold in the intestines. People who grow up drinking from infested waters may be immune to parasites they've already survived—Mexican citizens seldom contract Montezuma's revenge, while the incidence of tourists getting sick from drinking the water there is almost legendary. Even then,

Weighing in at around two pounds, a backpacker's water filtration outfit is a cheap way to guarantee no one present will become sick from aquatic parasites.

a strong, adapted immune system might be overwhelmed by high concentrations of pathogenic organisms. On the other hand, the chance of getting a parasite from ingesting small amounts of water while swimming is virtually nil.

Water Purification

Also confusing is the fact that much of what we do know about aquatic parasites has been discovered in recent years. The Vietnam War showed us—the hard way—that iodine and halazone (chlorine) tabs are ineffective against many parasites. In 1982 a rash of giardia occurred among hikers who drank untreated water from clear Rocky Mountain streams, and was made more dangerous because some doctors misdiagnosed the symptoms as a stomach flu. In

1998 it was discovered that iodine does not kill cryptosporidium. At the same time, a new cyst, cyclospora, was added to the roster of aquatic parasites, and it cannot be killed by iodine either.

Based on current knowledge, iodine is effective against bacteria (typhoid, cholera), flagellates (giardia), and viruses (hepatitis), but not cysts (cryptosporidium) or flatworms (tapeworms). Chlorine kills viruses and bacteria but not cysts or all flagellates. Tablets made from sodium chlorite and sodium dichloroisocyanurate dihydrate, like the Micropur MP1 tablets from Katadyn, have replaced chlorine and iodine. Each Micropur tab treats one liter of water, killing giardia, bacteria, and viruses within fifteen minutes, but a four-hour wait is required to ensure the demise of tough cysts.

The new electro-chemical purifier, like MSR's MiOx, also gets the job done. These gizmos use watch batteries to electrify a chamber filled with raw water and rock salt, converting those elements to chemicals that are safe for humans but deadly to pathogenic organisms. But, again, a four-hour wait time is needed to make sure all cysts are neutralized.

The most time-honored method of killing all aquatic pathogens is to bring the water they live in to a rolling boil and then boil it for one full minute. In fact, nearly every organism will be killed when water reaches 180 degrees Fahrenheit, but the boiling point of 212 degrees provides visual confirmation that the lethal temperature has been reached. Studies performed by the EPA show that even heat-resistant hepatitis viruses (rarely encountered in nature) are killed after boiling for one minute.

The downside of treating water with chemicals or with heat is that neither method removes harmful elements. Dead microscopic organisms are no longer infectious, but it is an unfortunate fact that many bodies of water are polluted with heavy metals, fertilizers, and pesticides that humans should not ingest. The best tool for addressing this problem is a backpacker-type water filter, as described in chapter 1, pp. 46–47. Some filters use a pumping action to force raw water through a cartridge, some do the same with a squeeze bottle, or just the force of gravity; some have ceramic filter cartridges, some are made from paper and fiberglass. All water filters are manufactured under strict EPA guidelines to remove bacteria, cysts, and flagellates, and also strain out up to 80 percent of harmful chemicals. They do not remove submicroscopic viruses, but these are seldom encountered away from civilization and are easily killed by adding chlorine or iodine.

Our understanding of waterborne pathogens has come a long way since whole settlements were decimated by typhoid and the days when trappers labeled all parasitic infections simply as "beaver fever." We know there are harmful bugs in every stream and lake and we know how to keep them from making us sick. Davy Crockett could only have wished for such an advantage.

Filtering drinking water through a hole chopped in the ice of a frozen lake.

The Solar Still

Water, water everywhere, and not a drop to drink. That lament of shipwrecked sailors throughout history exemplifies the difference between water and drinking water. In the navy's case, its life rafts are equipped with a solar still. This chambered ball-like device floats on a lanyard attached to the raft. Raw seawater in the still's reservoir is evaporated into water vapor by heat from sunlight then recombined into distilled water in a drinking reservoir. Salt and impurities are left behind when the evaporating water separates into gases, which rise to become channeled and cooled back to liquid form.

The same can be done on land, but be warned that the solar still is a relatively low-output device, especially on dry ground. The classic survivalist's model is a shallow hole with a drinking vessel in the center. The hole is covered by a large waterproof membrane (space blanket, plastic drop cloth), weighted in its center by a stone, directly over the cup, where it forms an inverted cone. Water gases evaporated from the warming ground soil rise and become trapped against the membrane, where they cool back into droplets, and run toward the lowest point—the stone—then collect and drip into the container below.

THE SOLAR STILL
(Shown in Cross Section)

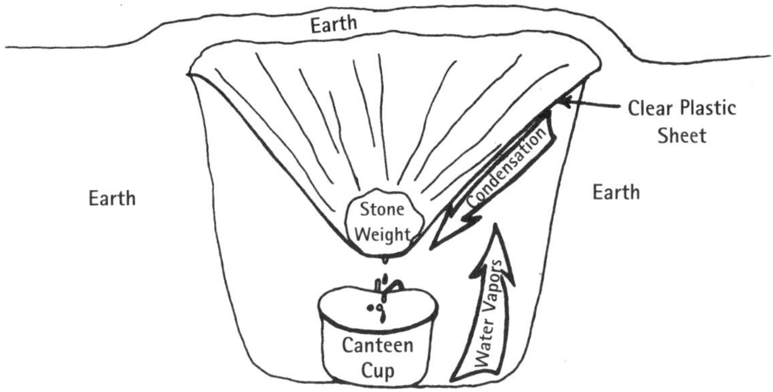

Earth

Clear Plastic Sheet

Earth

Condensation

Stone Weight

Earth

Water Vapors

Canteen Cup

The solar still has been tested pretty extensively. Tips for maximizing its efficiency include using a clear membrane that permits sunlight to pass through it to heat the earth below more quickly; black plastic is the least effective. Cover as large an area with the membrane as possible to collect as many droplets as possible. Urine, even alkali-poisoned water, can be poured into the bottom of the hole to increase evaporation. How well the solar still works also depends on how hot and sunny the weather is, as well as on the relative humidity.

The Condensation Still

A solar still is passive, reliant on sunlight and humidity levels, but a condensation still uses applied heat to actively evaporate contaminated water, forcing the vapors into an output where they recombine into drinking water.

Making a condensation still is as simple as filling a well-rinsed steel gasoline can with raw water, then placing the container over a small fire (sometimes just in the sun if the weather is hot). The can's pour spout or hose serves as an output for condensed water, but should be lengthened with an extension (garden) hose long enough to accommodate a loop. The loop traps particulates that might be forced into the hose by rising heat. In practice, a single condensation still can produce sufficient drinking water for several people, depending on the container size, and it can operate twenty-four hours a day so long as raw water and fire are available. Safety warnings include never heating water to a boil and never allowing the can to go dry, as either could cause unsafe pressures inside the container. If the container begins to bulge even slightly, remove it from heat immediately.

Water Sources

Few places in North America are completely devoid of water and none are without moisture in some form—the ability of a solar still to collect water from the air and ground is proof of that. But some water sources aren't obvious while others may not be wise to use. Freshwater springs are always a good bet when one needs clean drinking water. Springs are often plentiful in wooded lowlands, especially near streams. They can normally be found on ground several feet higher than the streams they feed into, and in many cases the source will be right in the side of a seemingly dry hill. Springs are always small and fast flowing, which precludes infestation by snails or other parasite carriers, and because the water is filtered through millions of tons of earth, rock, and gravel, the only impurities left in it are natural minerals. When taking water from a freshwater spring, always go to its point of origin, the place where it comes out of the ground. This water will be cold and clean enough to drink or cook with just as it is. The same may not hold true farther downstream, where waters are inevitably fed by runoff that passes over feces, and your chances of contracting a parasite increase exponentially.

Rain has always been a good water source, and it still is, although pollution and toxic emissions have added chemicals to it that it never contained before. Rainwater is at least as clean as urban tap water, and is definitely a safer bet than swamp water, so the survivalist should always be prepared to take advantage of this boon from above. The easiest method of collecting rainwater is to use a rubberized poncho or a plastic sheet set into a shallow depression in the ground. This will form a small watertight basin that can hold more than three gallons of water (a similar basin can be used for washing). Alternatively, you can suspend all the corners of your collection sheet to form a shelter and a runoff.

Snow is safe for use as drinking water, even though it contains the same chemical pollutants as modern rain. The biggest drawback to using melted snow as a source of water is that its volume is about three times as great as water; a gallon bucket filled with snow will yield just over a quart of water. Never eat snow if you feel cold, because it has a cooling effect on internal organs, and a slight chill can blossom into serious hypothermia. Always melt

Sometimes overlooked in cold weather, keeping well hydrated is as important to circulating warmed blood as it is to dissipating excess heat.

snow or ice with the campfire, and always try to drink warmed or hot water in freezing temperatures.

Dew is an often overlooked source of water in arid areas. Even the most sun-scorched desert has some degree of humidity, but during the heat of the day that moisture will be in the form of vapor. At night the cold cloudless skies that are the trademark of desert areas will do nothing to prevent the day's heat from escaping into the atmosphere, and temperatures will drop precipitously. The sudden drop in temperature will cause the water vapors to condense and gather on the surface of rocks where they can be collected with a dog rag (see chapter 1, pp. 49–50). When the dog rag becomes saturated with dew, simply wring it out into the canteen cup—or directly into your mouth—and gather more. Dewfall is typically at its maximum from 3:00 a.m. to sunrise.

Like people, plants need water to live, and their tissues contain a large percentage of water. Probably all of us have heard about how aboriginal peoples obtained liquid from jungle lianas, desert cacti, or underground tubers, but the truth is that all nontoxic soft-bodied plants and their roots can be used to provide a thirst-quenching (if usually bitter) juice. To obtain liquid from a plant, first crush it between the palms with a rolling action, as if rolling clay into a ball. When the plant takes on a wet, fibrous consistency raise the hand slightly overhead, tip your head back, point your extended thumb at your open mouth and squeeze hard. The juices forced from the crushed plant will flow downward to drip off the end of your thumb and into your mouth.

The same can be done with roots, but as they're harder they will usually need to be reduced to a pile of shavings with your knife before any liquid can be squeezed from them using hand pressure. When traveling through an arid environment, bear in mind that some species of plants die back after the rainy season, but the roots will remain viable and are often a good source of water. A withered plant lying on the surface of the ground or an apparently dead twig sticking up may indicate a live, dormant root beneath the surface. But always use caution and never drink liquid from any plant that you can't positively identify as nontoxic.

Knowing the location of active water holes is absolutely vital to anyone traveling through desert country. As a service to travelers, desert states maintain a number of water tanks and wind-powered well pumps in the backcountry. Maps giving the location of each of these are available from state fish and game agencies and anyone driving, hiking, or riding through the desert should have one for area. It's also a good idea to begin the journey with as much water as you can carry, just in case.

Squeezing water from a plant.

The water from a stranded vehicle's radiator can be used as a source of drinking water, but only after distillation. Never, ever even taste the water from the cooling system of any vehicle as it comes out of the radiator. Triethylene glycol, the active ingredient in antifreeze/coolant is extremely toxic, and ingesting even small amounts of it can cause immediate kidney failure, convulsions, and death. The solar still and condensation still are capable of purifying the coolant into drinking water by separating water vapors from the heavier glycol, but I recommend double-distillation with something as toxic as antifreeze. Note that a backpacker-type water filter, despite removing 80 percent of chemicals and metals, does not make engine coolant safe to drink.

Survival Tips

As mentioned earlier, never try to conserve water through abstinence; the best place to transport water is in your body. Fainting is a symptom of heat exhaustion, and a person who passes out in the heat of a midday desert might never wake up again. The job of a canteen or water bottle is to carry excess water until you become thirsty.

Carrying two pebbles in the mouth is an old Apache method of warding off thirst. The pebbles fool the mouth into thinking that it has something edible, which causes the saliva to flow and keeps the mouth from drying out. Chewing gum will do the same thing, but since sugar or artificial sweeteners increase feelings of thirst, gum used to keep the mouth moist should be chewed well after the flavor is gone. But remember, placing an object in the mouth will only help to stave off the feeling of thirst; it does nothing to replenish water lost through perspiration, and it will not prevent dehydration.

Night travel is always recommended when going through desert country on foot. Even slight exertion in temperatures that can top one hundred degrees Fahrenheit will cause you to perspire heavily, and seriously deplete your body's onboard water supply. Conversely, the cloudless sky will allow the heat of the day to dissipate rapidly after sunset, with temperatures sometimes falling to the freezing mark. Since the nights are too cold to sleep and the days too hot to walk, the survivalist should always travel at night, holing up in a shady spot during the day.

If shade isn't available, it can be created. Chapter 2 describes how to suspend a space blanket or poncho between two poles, like a lean-to, to create a shaded sleeping area (see pp. 72–74). This is probably the best hot-weather shelter in open desert, but erecting it requires a minimum of two poles. In sand or rock, where only low scrub can survive, these may be impossible to come by. When that's the case, a shaded shelter can be created by finding or excavating a shallow, body-length trench in the ground or between two rock outcroppings and stretching the space blanket, shiny side up, across it. The ends on either side of the trench can be held in place by weighting them with rocks or just burying them in the sand. Both ends of the finished shelter should be left open to allow the circulation of as much air as possible. The reflective surface of the space blanket will throw back a large portion of the sun's heat, and the area under the shelter will remain about ten degrees cooler than the outside. The shelter will also stick out like a sore thumb to any plane passing within five miles.

The latest in personal water transport, collapsible bladders that roll up to fit into a pocket when empty have proved their worth in recent years.

A survivalist traveling through barren country will want to carry as much water as possible and to make the most of any water holes encountered on the journey back to civilization. For this reason I recommend having two canteens in the survival kit. Additional water can be carried in makeshift canteens, the number and type of which are limited only by imagination and available resources. Perhaps the best emergency canteen is the resealable soft drink bottle. Ordinary screw-cap jars make good emergency canteens too. Plastic bags will also work, but since few of these are watertight, the best way to carry water in them is to fill them with saturated cloth, paper, or foam rubber from a vehicle's seats. The absorbent material will retain water while the plastic bag will help to keep it from evaporating. A small drinking hole can be poked through the bag at one corner, and the water recovered by squeezing trapped water directly into the mouth.

When you come upon a water hole, stream, or any other body of water in hot, arid country, never lie on your belly to drink from it, and absolutely never throw yourself into the water with the wild abandon depicted in Hollywood movies. A sudden cooling of the

COYOTE TRACKS

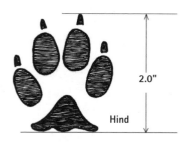

2.0"

Hind

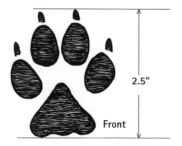

2.5"

Front

Found throughout the Americas, the presence of coyotes can be beneficial to a survivalist; these consummate scavengers make obvious trails to water holes, especially in the desert, and they are a sign that small prey is available.

body after exposing it to hours of heat and dehydration can cause a state of shock severe enough to cause unconsciousness. It's one of life's bitter ironies that people dying of thirst in the desert have found water only to drown in it. The safest way of drinking directly from a water hole or stream is to kneel and use a cupped hand or canteen cup to raise it to the mouth.

Coyotes and jackrabbits are the most numerous mammals in barren country. Rabbits and most reptiles can obtain sufficient moisture from their food to live, but coyotes need to drink regularly, usually in the early morning and late afternoon. Following an established coyote trail a few hundred yards might lead you to a water hole, and it should be visible from a distance because coyotes like to survey a place before revealing themselves. Thirsty animals can smell water for long distances, and the survivalist traveling with a horse, burro, or dog can find water simply by giving his animal its head and following. But keep in mind that some desert water holes contain toxic levels of alkali. Use the solar still to purify any suspicious water before drinking it.

FIVE

Food

Food has always been a priority among primitive peoples; it was an element of their lives that was often unpredictable, and always subject to the whims of nature. Rituals were conducted to appeal to the spirits responsible for bringing in the buffalo, creating rain, or initiating the spawning run of migratory fish, but appealing to the spirits has never been very effective, so it was the duty of every tribal member to be an opportunistic hunter and gatherer. Many methods employed by the Indians to take wild game, fish, and fowl were so effective that they've been outlawed in the United States and Canada, but both of these countries recognize the right to harvest food in an emergency.

Common Edible Plants

Wild plants are generally the most dependable food source. The majority of nutrients necessary to sustain human life can be obtained from plants alone, but as the Indians and mountain men of old were aware, meat is important for a balanced diet in a high-demand environment. Most plants are edible in terms of nontoxicity, but some of those that are considered edible are neither palatable nor digestible. And some of those that are very nutritious and digestible taste terrible. This chapter will cover only those plants that are easily recognized, widespread, nutritious, and tolerable to the human taste buds. Plants that have a short growing season, are limited to specific areas, or require boiling in several changes of water to remove their toxins won't be mentioned here. Mushrooms will be entirely ignored because they contribute little in the way

The bracken fern fiddleheads have matured beyond edibility, but the blueberries, serviceberries, raspberries, and goldthread berries are among the natural delectables that have taken their place across America.

Wintergreen berries are a spring delicacy in northern conifer forests (they're also a good remedy for a sour stomach), but they are never abundant; a survivor should be prepared to take sustenance from many sources, which also helps to ensure a balanced diet.

of nutrition and are sometimes difficult to recognize, and certain species are lethal if eaten. The wild vegetables covered in this book represent only a small fraction of all edible wild plants. For those who want to include a more comprehensive catalog of wild plants in their survival kit, I recommend *North American Wildlife* (Reader's Digest, 1982) and *Edible Wild Plants,* by Oliver Perry Medsger (latest edition Oliver Press, 2007).

Reindeer moss (*Cladonia rangiferina*) is an easily recognizable member of the lichen family common to every continent on earth. Many species of lichen (hybrid plants that are half algae, half fungus) are found throughout the world, and most are not only edible (after boiling) but contain nearly all of the nutrition required to keep a human healthy. Many a stranded explorer has survived a prolonged stay in the wilderness by eating these lowly plants; the most famous case was during World War II in the winter of 1943, when Norwegian commandos were dropped into Nazi-held territory and were forced to subsist on a diet of mostly reindeer moss until spring. The Nazis had all but given the commandos up for dead, but they were healthy enough to complete their mission of blowing up a heavy water plant, which was Germany's chance of beating the Allies to the atomic bomb.

REINDEER MOSS

Found in open areas in northern regions all over the world. Member of lichen family. Grows from two to four inches tall. Color ranges from gray to green to blue. Dry and crunchy when dehydrated. Contains stimulant, antibiotic, protein, sugar, and a laxative when eaten raw. Usually grows in thick clusters or "carpets."

Reindeer moss is easy to recognize. It prefers sandy, open meadows and fields where it grows in carpetlike masses of dull blue, green, or gray that may extend for several yards in all directions. Individual plants will range from two to four inches high. During dry weather these carpets will be brittle and crunchy underfoot, changing quickly to a spongy mass in the lightest rain. Reindeer moss and other lichens should always be cooked before eating because many of them contain a potent laxative that is destroyed by boiling or baking. Other ingredients that are not destroyed by cooking include a high sugar content, most vitamins, most minerals, and a broad-spectrum antibiotic similar to penicillin. Canadian sourdoughs are reported to make a stimulating tea by boiling a strong concentration of crushed reindeer moss in water. I've tried this tea and the light-headed feeling it gave me was anything but stimulating. Reindeer moss can be prepared as a food by boiling it for ten minutes and eating it right out of the cook pot, but the most common method of preparation is to boil it, mash it into a paste, then bake it into cakes on a hot rock. Eskimo hunters once ate reindeer moss directly from the first stomach of freshly killed caribou. This dish is known as "Eskimo salad," and although I haven't tried it, I'm sure it isn't an improvement on the taste of baked lichen cakes.

Plantains are one of the most common weeds on the North American continent, and at least one species is found everywhere from the tip of Alaska to Central America. Common plantain (*Plantago major*) can be found growing in swamps, fields, manicured lawns, gravel driveways, and through cracks in sidewalks. This tenacious plant is the bane of modern gardeners and suburbanites because it can be cut to the ground only to reappear again within forty-eight hours. Ironically, it was once highly prized as a food plant. The leaves are richer in vitamin A, C, and iron than spinach, and its seedpods contain several of the B vitamins. Plantains are easily recognizable anywhere they grow, and the entire plant may be eaten raw or boiled as a potherb. The texture is a bit tough and

COMMON PLANTAIN

Grows two to twenty inches tall and looks similar to small rhubarb plant. Leaves tasty and nutritious, richer in iron and vitamins A and C than spinach. Seedpods are green with pinkish flower, and are a good source of vitamin B. Grows everywhere from fields to cracks in city sidewalks. In bloom from April to October. Found all over North American continent.

Originally brought to America from Europe to serve as a fast-growing vegetable, common plantain is found everywhere in America; crushed leaves reduce swelling in insect bites and stings, seedpods are rich in B vitamins, and leaves have more A, C, and iron than plantain's close cousin, spinach.

the leaves are stringy, so I recommend boiling the plant until tender. The taste is a bit bland, but not at all unpleasant. Plantains can be found everywhere from April until the winter snows cover them.

Queen Anne's lace (*Daucus carota*) is the most common member of the wild carrot family. Its tall stems, with their frilly white

QUEEN ANNE'S LACE

Found in open meadows and fields. Grows up to five feet tall with white umbrella flowers. Edible white taproot smells strongly of carrots. Very similar to the highly toxic hemlock plant except hemlock lacks carrot odor.

121

umbels (multilobed flower heads), can be seen in every open field, pasture, and abandoned lot on the continent from May through October. The vertical leaves are frilly and even a bit scraggly, and the center of the umbel is dotted with a single, dark-colored flower. There is some danger of confusing this plant with the very similar, very toxic poison hemlock (*Conium maculatum*), but positive identification can be made by smelling the root: Queen Anne's lace and its relatives have a strong odor of carrots, hemlock does not.

Watercress (*Nasturtium officinale*) is the survivalist's best, and sometimes only, source of fresh greens in the winter. It grows in running fresh water almost everywhere in the world, and when snow covers the ground it will be the only leafy green plant found in streams, rivers, and springs. In summer it can be found growing in thick green carpets that sometimes choke smaller streams. The small clusters of tiny four-petaled flowers bloom from March to November, rising vertically from the surface of the water on slender stalks and ranging in color from white to light pink.

WATERCRESS

Vinelike growth forms up to ten feet long. Small, white four-petal flowers bloom from March to November. Leaves are dark, shiny green, and divided into many leaflets. May be found in nearly any freshwater and stream at all times of the year, sometimes growing so densely it resembles a solid mass. Often creeps up on stream banks during the summer months. Should be thoroughly washed before eating.

Watercress has long been sold commercially as a low-calorie, vitamin-rich vegetable. Eaten raw, it has a tangy, pungent taste faintly reminiscent of horseradish, but since its vinelike growth form is a favored browsing place for parasite-carrying freshwater snails, I recommend that it be boiled before eating, or at least washed very thoroughly.

Cattails (*Typha latifolia*) are a source of wild food at water's edge every month of the year—no survivalist need ever go hungry where these plants grow. The tall reedlike growth form, with vertical green leaves that resemble giant blades of grass, is familiar to most people. The plants can be found growing in ditches, marshes, along stream banks, and almost anywhere else freshwater is found. The edible parts of the cattail plant are the root, the core of the young shoots, the immature green seed head, and thick yellow pollen shaken from the spike atop the mature brown seed head. Young shoots begin to sprout in early spring, sometimes pushing their way upward through snow. These can be snapped off just below the surface of the ground and the white core eaten raw after the stringy green leaves have been stripped away, or they can be boiled briefly to make a dish known as "Russian asparagus." The raw shoots are crispy and pleasant to eat, with a flavor that I can only describe as a cross between celery and water chestnuts.

The rootstocks of the cattail can be eaten raw or boiled any time of the year. Some have likened them to potatoes, but the similarity is limited to the fact that both of them contain starch. Cattail

COMMON CATTAIL

Grows two to ten feet tall. In bloom from May to July. Has starchy edible root. Tender young shoots may be prepared by boiling or steaming like asparagus. Basal portion of stem may be eaten raw. Found in marshes, ditches, and along lakeshores and riverbanks. Leaves inedible, but may be woven into mats, blankets, and other items.

Where there is permanent fresh water, there will probably be cattails growing in the shallows.

roots have a tough outer bark and a fibrous, woody texture that bears little resemblance to the soft, fleshy potato. They are nutritious and generally palatable after boiling, although some may find the high starch content objectionable. Probably the best way to prepare them as a survival food is to use the same method as the Indians of old: Simply roast or boil the roots for a half hour, then chew them, swallowing what seems edible, and spit out the woody parts. Green boiled seed heads were also eaten by the American Indians who roasted or boiled them and then ate the cooked fruits like corn on the cob. The flesh is reportedly nutritious and digestible, but the taste and texture are only tolerable.

From May to July the male cattail plants produce large pollen-bearing spikes that sit on top of the mature seed head. Large amounts of pollen can be gathered in a relatively short time by using a stick to knock the powder into a bush hat or similar container. When enough of the powder has been collected, it can be mixed with a little water, stirred into a thick batter, and made into "pollen cookies" by spreading the mixture thinly over a hot rock or mess tin. A couple of turtle or bird eggs will enhance the taste and texture.

Violets (*Viola*) are an abundant, nutritious, and very palatable wild vegetable that should never be overlooked in warm weather. More than sixty species grow in North America; some have violet flowers, some white, some yellow, and at least one species is pink. Regardless of the color of the flower, all species are edible, although the downy yellow violet may cause a mild case of diarrhea if eaten raw.

CANADA VIOLET

Most common of the more than sixty species of violet in North America. White flowers with five petals. Toothed leaves. Entire plant is edible and tasty, raw or cooked as a potherb. Flowers taste sweet. May grow up to eighteen inches tall.

The most common species of violet in the forests of the United States and Canada are the common blue violet (*Viola sororia*), arrowleaf violet (*Viola sagittata*), white violet (*Viola macloskeyi*), Canada violet (*Viola canadensis*), and downy yellow violet (*Viola pubescens*). The leaves are generally heart shaped, but in a few cases they resemble the scraggly multilobed leaves of the toxic buttercup. For this reason I recommend avoiding any violet that doesn't have heart-shaped leaves, especially if no flower is present. All violets in bloom will have five petals, and the two top petals will almost always stand vertically together above the other three. The bottommost petal will point downward and will be marked by a number of raylike lines spreading from the center of the flower in all directions. Flowers stand above the plant on their own stems, and each of the leaf stems support only one leaf. Plant sizes vary with species but typically range from two to twelve inches tall. Most violets can be found growing almost anywhere, but all of them prefer moist or even wet soil. The white violet especially prefers swamps and marshes. The entire violet plant may be eaten raw or boiled as a potherb, and the flowers are a good source of raw sugar. The uncooked leaves and stems have a mild, pleasant taste that's hard to distinguish from raw lettuce.

Burdock (*Arctium minus*) is a familiar plant; only Alaska and the extreme north territories of Canada are beyond the range of this hardy weed. A thornless relative of thistles, burdock grows to a height of five feet and is common to fields, abandoned lots, open woods, and stream banks throughout its range. Immature first-year plants resemble a fuzzy-leafed rhubarb plant, and the purple-tufted burs of the mature growth can be seen rising above the surrounding grasses in open fields. The leaves, stems, and root of the burdock plant are all edible, but only the large, deeply-buried root is actually palatable. Some old-timers say that the fleshy stems can be peeled and boiled or eaten raw, but my experience is that, even with the bitter rind removed, the taste is sufficient to cause an

COMMON BURDOCK

Nearly all parts edible: starchy taproot (the most palatable part), tender young leaves, stems, and basal leafstalks that can be peeled and eaten raw or boiled. In bloom from July to October. Found in fields, vacant lots, pastures, and nearly any other open place. Looks very much like rhubarb before flowering. Found all over North American continent.

involuntary grimace. The young leaves are also said to be good as a potherb, but these too are very bitter.

Fishing

Drop a polished woodsman into a place that has permanent water, and he or she will probably not go hungry. Throughout history humans have been fueled by a diet of fish and other seafood, and fishing cultures around the globe have invented a multitude of methods for catching marine animals.

Some of these techniques are not legal in some places; in fact, this usually confirms that the outlawed method is a bit too effective.

Fishing Bait

A few fish—like creek chubs in summer—are ravenous enough to attack a naked hook, but most need enticement. Earthworms dug from damp riverbanks or from under wet leaves are among the best baits, along with grasshoppers and most other insects, pieces of clam or frog, even pieces of fish.

Many hikers already carry fish bait. Raisins appeal to a variety of fish, probably because of the sugars they contain—all animals need calories. Chunks of summer sausage have proved to be very good bait for all types of fish (including a few trophy-size northern pike). Even gummy bears have been used to catch fish, with sometimes impressive results on spawning steelhead.

Aggressive fish, like pike, walleye, and trout, might be visually tempted into grabbing a hook that offers no food value, so long as it has been decorated to excite a fish's hunting instinct. Trout fishermen have landed nice catches using nothing more than a few inches of red, orange, or yellow yarn tied to a hook and floated on the surface. Colored foam earplugs threaded onto long-shank hooks have caught surface-feeding bass and trout. Bottom-feeding species, like catfish and suckers (and turtles), have been caught for generations with a few inches of shoelace soaked in bacon grease. Other natural baits that have proved effective include discarded feathers, fur, or your own hair tied onto a hook to form a fly, and at least one large-mouthed bass has gone for a dandelion floated on the water.

Handfishing

Catching fish using only one's hands is, almost ironically, illegal in some places. Spawning fish that congregate seasonally in flowing waters—suckers, trout, and humpback salmon in spring, pike in early summer, chinook salmon in the fall—are especially good prey for handfishing. Typically, fish of every species will scatter at your approach, taking refuge under sunken logs, stumps, and undercut stream banks, where they feel protected.

Handfishing, accomplished entirely by feel, can be done day or night, making it a natural for military survival. The technique is to simply lay your open hand flat, palm up, against the stream bottom, then slide it into likely hiding spots. A hand sliding along the bottom seldom disturbs sheltered fish. When you feel a fish's belly against your palm, close your hand hard around its body, driving your fingertips into its flesh. Immediately arc the hand containing the fish toward the nearest bank, tossing your catch far enough inland to ensure that it can't flop back into the water. Do not try to hold on to a flopping fish's body or you'll probably lose it.

Spearfishing

Spearing is an effective means of obtaining fish in shallow water. Multiple prongs enable the spear to be deadly over a greater area, increasing the chances that each lunge will net a fish. Prongs should be barbed, to help keep skewered fish in place.

A working spearhead can be whittled from the crotch of a green sapling, particularly one that branches in three directions, but be sure that the tines are stout enough to pierce and hold a fighting fish (usually about a half inch in diameter). Barbs can be whittled into the wood and then hardened by charring the green tines in a fire.

The steel four-tine frog spearhead found at department stores for under five dollars is better.

The head is easily friction-fitted to a handle that can be cut on the spot in most places, and it will suffice to take fish more than a foot long yet is small enough to be effective on smaller fish, even crayfish, snakes, and rabbits hiding in their burrows.

Again, spawning fish offer the most opportunities to spear dinner, but river and lake fish can be speared from undercut banks and other hiding spots. Bring the spearhead as close to the fish's body as possible before lunging hard to drive the prey against the stream bottom. Hold it tightly against the streambed until it wiggles weakly, then toss spear and all onto shore with one motion.

In lakes and ponds, larger bass tend toward darker, cooler deep spots until sunset, when they emerge to hunt. The approach of these lunkers is telegraphed by an abundance of minnows and crayfish scurrying almost onto the beach where large fish can't reach them. Where the minnows school most heavily may result in seeing several meal-size predator fish. The fish will be wary of moving profiles against the sky, so it pays to have a long spear shaft that can reach out from cover.

Fish can also be speared through the ice of frozen lakes. Many inland lakes are home sometimes to large pike and other fish that can be speared through an ice hole even in waist-deep water.

Chumming the water with pieces of clams that gravitate to shallow water in winter, or with the innards of caught fish, helps to ensure that hungry fish pass under your hole.

Knife Fishing

More effective than some would like it to be, knife fishing has taken many a large salmon, trout, or pike during their spawning runs up rivers and streams. Spawning is hard work, and often an exhausted fish caught up in the activity will ignore a person who approaches it slowly, knife held low in a tight fist, ready to stab forward. The cutting edge should be held upward, because when the blade penetrates as far as it can into the fish's body, just below the spine and directly behind the gill, you should raise the knife upward, as though trying to lift the fish out of the water. In most cases the fish will fall free, back into the water but will be too badly wounded to swim more than a few yards without turning belly up.

Hand-Lining

Hand-lining is the simplest hook-and-line method. Tie a fishing line securely to a baited hook with a fisherman's knot, weighted as necessary, and toss it into a likely fishing hole while holding on to the loose end of the line. When a fish grabs the bait, the force from the pull it exerts is transferred through the line to the hand

Where there is permanent water, there are probably fish, and a pocket fishing kit should be considered a necessary survival item.

of the angler, who can react quickly with a short counterjerk to set the barbed hook firmly into the prey's flesh. Once hooked, the fish is retrieved by pulling in the line hand over hand and onto shore. Avoid lifting fish larger than pan size out of the water by the line; drag them onto shore, because a hard flop can snap a line that is rated several times the fish's actual weight.

When not in use, a handline is probably most easily carried by winding it "hook, line, and sinker," around a six-inch section of a dead branch, one or two inches in diameter. The hook point can be embedded into the wood to make it safer to carry. In fact, several of these instantly deployable fishing outfits can be carried in a pocket, which is good for a plane-crash survivor who is trekking back to civilization and must make camp each evening. Alternatively, these lines can be fastened to a fresh-cut fishing pole, or rigged into a trigger line trap (described on pp. 132–34).

Pole Fishing

We can't know who first conceived of using a simple crane to extend a fishing line away from an angler, but the fishing pole has been in use worldwide for a long time. Today's precision-made casting outfits are sometimes things of beauty, but the concept of reaching out with a baited hook can be accomplished using a springy green sapling (usually willow or dogwood found growing on the shoreline), about six feet long, with roughly eight feet of fishing line tied to its narrow end.

Other advantages of the fishing pole include enhanced sensitivity that enables an angler to feel activity at the hook, and a shock-absorber effect that prevents hooked fish from getting a solid pull as they fight.

Fishing poles can also be short. A two-foot branch of springy cedar has landed many dinners of brook trout in places too restrictive for a full-length pole. Likewise, an ice fisherman angling through a hole on a frozen lake needs to be almost on top of his line, keeping back just far enough to avoid being seen from below.

The Trigger Line

With most of our planet underwater, fish have been a part of the human diet since before recorded history. Almost any permanent body of water can be presumed to support fish, and virtually all species are edible.

The challenge has always been getting fish from the water so they can be rendered into food. In a real-life backwoods scenario where fish might provide most or all of the calories a person ingests, you need a technique that produces maximum results with minimal effort. Pan-size fish are most numerous and easily caught, but catching these morsels one at a time on a conventional rod and reel may be too slow to keep in step with caloric demands, especially for a group.

The trigger line, taught to me by my Ojibwa grandfather Amos Wasageshik when I was a boy, is one of the simplest and most effective methods of harvesting fish for survival. Part spring snare, part fishing pole, a trigger line automatically sets its hook in a fish's mouth when it takes the bait. Once hooked, the fish remains at the end of the line, alive but securely caught, until retrieved. Even better, trigger lines will catch and hold fish while you spend valuable energy and time doing other things.

The working principles of a trigger line are simple. Required materials for a single set are one fishhook, one or two split-shot sinkers, about ten feet of at least six-pound test monofilament fishing line, a springy green sapling, and a stout stake chopped from dead wood. Since more sets usually equal more fish, the fishing kit that resides permanently in my own day pack contains a fifty-yard spool of fishing line, two dozen assorted sinkers, and one hundred assorted fishhooks safely contained inside a capped plastic bottle.

The stake functions as an anchor for the springy pole and is best made from dry dead wood because it can be notched more cleanly with a knife than green wood. An ideal candidate will be about ten inches long by two inches in diameter. Sharpen the end that will be pushed into the ground, then cut a sharp-edged notch (see illustration on p. 134) about halfway through one side about two inches below the top end. Drill or pound the stake to a depth of about six inches into the edge of a stream bank. The notch should always point downstream, or away from shore in the case of ponds and lakes, because those are the directions a biting fish will probably take the bait.

Next, rig the pole, which should be made from a springy green sapling (usually common on stream banks) about three feet long and with a base of about one inch. Tie on the line about two inches from the pole's narrow end with a fisherman's slipknot, attach hook and sinkers, then drive the butt end of the pole firmly into the ground about two feet inshore from the stake.

Next, bend the pole downward and wedge it into the stake's notch. The idea is to restrain the pole under tension, but not so securely that it won't slip free with a light tug on the line. Techniques for achieving a

Setting the trigger line under tension into the anchor stake notch.

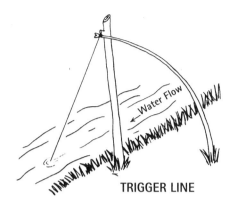

TRIGGER LINE

perfect fit include slightly flattening the upper side of the pole with a knife, deepening the notch, or angling the anchor stake.

When an ideal fit is achieved, bait the hook with a worm, grasshopper, or even a chunk of summer sausage, and toss it away from shore, being sure there is as little slack in the line as possible. A fish tugging against the baited hook will pull the pole from its restraining notch, causing it to spring forcefully in a direction opposite the fish, driving the hook's barbed point deep into flesh in the fish's mouth. The fish will remain there, tethered to shore, until retrieved or released by the angler.

Tips for making the trigger line work more efficiently include knowing what types of fish are likely to be caught and then setting the trap accordingly. Northern pike spawn upriver in May, and their sharp teeth require a steel leader; bullheads and catfish forage close to the bottom and tend to tug gently against a hook; bass and brook trout hit a bait violently. Long-shank hooks are more easily removed from your catch's mouth, and smaller hooks can catch big fish, but large hooks will be stripped of bait by fish too small to swallow them.

Fish Traps

Fish must travel in water, a fact that has been exploited by terrestrial animals forever, from salmon-fishing grizzlies to panfish-

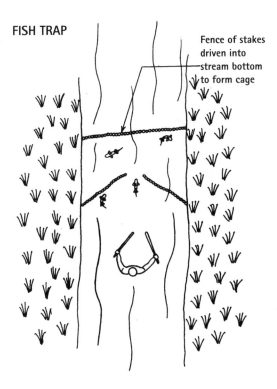

FISH TRAP

Fence of stakes driven into stream bottom to form cage

eating otters. The trick is to find, or to get, fish into a place where the water is shallow or the pathway restricted, and you have the advantage as a predator. Tidal pools have always been harvested for trapped fish by aboriginal peoples, and spawning fish intent on getting upstream can be found in, or diverted into, narrow tributaries.

To help channel fish into a suitable killing pool, a fence of tightly spaced wooden stakes can be driven into the bottom, and fish herded through the opening. A pair of long sticks held in either hand increases the area you can cover while herding fish into the trap.

Bowfishing

Bowfishing is as old as the bow and arrow and it is one of the more effective means of taking pan-size and larger fish. Ideally, the fisherman does not shoot the arrow more than a foot, and no fletching is required. Arrows for bowfishing are much longer than hunting arrows—about five feet—to enable a concealed survivalist to place the sharpened, barbed, and fire-hardened point within inches of a submerged fish's body. Because of refraction it is essential that the arrow's tip be underwater to make accurate shots, and point of aim should always be the center body, straight in, and clean through the body. This will not kill the fish; being skewered on a long pole only cripples the prey, and you must move quickly to secure it before the fish can wriggle free or flop into deeper water. Placing a foot on the arrow shaft pins the fish to the bottom, while you get a pair of fingers securely through its gills.

Suitable bow staves and arrow shafts can usually be found growing in the same places where they will be used. Green willow makes a great bow stave; select a sapling that is at least one inch in diameter (thicker equals more power, but more strength is needed to draw the bow) and relatively straight over a distance of six, even seven, feet. A fishing bow is extra long because it shoots a longer missile and needs a longer power stroke. Remember that you might need to hold the bow drawn for several minutes when actually fishing; it needs only enough force to drive an arrow completely through the body of its prey.

Woven plant fibers do not make a good bowstring, and rawhide—which is only slightly better—is not easily surrendered by animals who wear it. Drawstrings from jackets and laces from shoes make good bowstrings, but this is one of those foreseeable needs that every hiker should be prepared to meet with several lengths of different-size cord in a survival kit; the weight is nothing, but the value is potentially life saving. Tie the string securely to one end of the bow stave, going first over the top of the end, then wrapping the string around a dozen times—these wraps will pull tighter under force. Tie off the end with a series of hitches.

Place the tied end downward, against the outside of one foot. Step in front of the bow stave with your opposite leg, so that pressing forward on the upper end flexes the center of the stave against the back of your thigh. Flex the stave a few inches, until the taut string is about eight inches from the bow's center, and tie it off with the same method used for the opposite end.

Bowfishing arrows are equally simple. You should have at least two. Straight green dogwood, willow, or cedar shoots growing at water's edge are among the good candidates for an arrow shaft, which should be at least five feet long and stout but not too heavy to handle comfortably. Shave the outside of each shaft with a knife (or chip of stone) until they are barkfree and as smooth as you can make them. Carefully whittle a wedge-shaped "nock" into the butt of the arrow shaft to accommodate the bowstring. Sharpen the business end to a keen point, and cut small forward-pointing wedges from around the point to make it barbed and not easy to pull from flesh. If possible, harden the tips by charring them in fire, then scrape each to a finished point that will pierce easily. When fishing, arrows can be tied off with several feet of line to a piece of dead wood that will serve as a fishing float to mark the fish's location, if it should escape from sight.

Firearm Fishing

Firearm fishing is illegal in most states, largely because a gun in the wrong hands can decimate whole runs of spawning salmon and trout at sandbars and other shallows where large fish must wriggle through, bellies scraping and dorsal fins well above water. A .22-caliber expanding bullet, like Remington's Yellowjacket, fired from a rifle or pistol through the spine of a large fish will cause it to thrash uncontrollably. Then, it will typically zoom off in a straight line, inevitably encountering a bank or shore, where it will expire. On winding streams, all a survivalist has to do is retrieve supper from the shoreline.

If necessary, a .22 can kill fish that are six inches below water. Do remember to account for refraction; aim for the largest mass, and aim low, below the fish. Try to shoot straight down into the water, and be ready to stop wounded fish with a second shot.

Fish Snares

Several yards of baling wire in a compact coil have been a normal part of my backcountry outfit for decades. The wire breaks easily enough yet works for wire ties, large makeshift needles, and a host of other uses.

More serious uses for baling wire include using it in a spring snare to virtually decapitate deer, or as a fishing snare for large fish, such as spawning pike, salmon, or trout. Begin by forming a loop at one end and winding the free end of the wire around it a dozen times to secure it with a form that looks something like a small hangman's knot. Feed the opposite end of the wire through this loop to form a second, larger loop that is the actual noose. With the noose open to a diameter of two feet, fasten the free end to a stout (about two inches) stave, about five feet long, leaving about a foot of wire between the stave and the noose.

In practice, the pole is used to reach out and slowly slide the noose over a fish's body. When the noose is midway on the fish's body, a hard upward yank draws it tightly around the flesh, sinking more deeply as the fish struggles. Maintain a hard upward pressure—do not lift the fish into the air, or it may slip free—and drag your prize onto shore.

Cleaning Fish

Basic fish cleaning is simple enough to master on the first try. Do not bother scaling or skinning, as the skin will slide off after cooking. Make a cut with your knife or sharpened rock from the anus hole near the underside of the fish's tail to its gills. Remove the entrails from the body cavity and pull out the gills by hooking a finger through them, if you desire. Finally, wash the fish, and it is ready for cooking.

Cooking Fish

Fish must be cooked before eating. That isn't an antisushi sentiment, but practical advice for avoiding infestation by parasites that might be contained in fish flesh. One thing worse than being in a survival situation is being in a survival situation with diarrhea and vomiting.

There are many methods for cooking fish under survival circumstances: Some say you should wrap it in layers of large green leaves (like an ear of corn), or maybe coat it with mud before tossing it onto a low fire. The most expedient method is to simply bend the cleaned fish into a U shape, and skewer it at both ends with a sharpened stick. Held thus, the fish can be cooked evenly over a low fire until the flesh becomes flaky and white and comes cleanly away from bone, and the skin peels away easily. The most common mistake is trying to cook the meat too fast over too hot a fire, so pick at the cooking meat from time to time to see if it flakes away.

The faster you can get a fish from water to fire, the better it will taste. Unfortunately, cooked or raw, fish can spoil overnight in warm weather. A solution for giving fish meat a longer edible life is to dry it as thoroughly as possible, driving out moisture that most bacteria need to thrive.

Alternatively, you can smoke your fish by hanging the flesh over the fire pit within a tepeelike frame, which is then mostly enclosed with sections of bark stripped from dead trees or green foliage—anything that will help to contain drying smoke. The fish

Basic campfire cooking can consist of no more than a fish fillet (shown) spitted onto a long green branch, and roasted like a hot dog.

is done, and preserved for the next week, when the flesh is completely dry and peels away in strips. Green wood atop a hot bed of coals is best for smoking, but avoid green pine that can impart a turpentine taste to the meat.

Other Aquatic Animals
Crayfish

Crayfish (Astacidea family) are common to freshwaters throughout North America. Resembling miniature lobsters, crayfish reach an adult length of five inches and are available as food from spring until they hibernate in the muddy bottom of freshwater in the fall. The easiest way to gather crayfish is to dangle a small piece of fish, clam, or even a worm on a fishhook in front of the underwater crevices where they hide during daylight. The crayfish will dart out to grab the morsel in a powerful claw so tenaciously that it will usually not be able to release its grip before being pulled from the water.

These nocturnal crustaceans can also be gathered at night by blinding them with a flashlight in the shallow water where they feed and then simply plucking them off the bottom. Shine the light at the crayfish's eyes, which causes it to stop, claws up and open in a defensive position. Then, simply reach around it from behind and pluck it from the bottom between your thumb and forefinger.

Crayfish tails can be skewered and cooked over fire, but the most popular cooking method is to drop them alive into boiling water, which kills them instantly. The crayfish is ready to eat in five minutes, and like the larger lobster, their shells will turn a brilliant red or orange. The meat inside the tail and claws is especially good, and some Cajuns have even been known to suck the salty juices from inside the body after the tail has been twisted off.

Turtles

Turtles are a good source of meat when you are near water, if they're large enough to be worth the effort. The most common of these is the snapping turtle (*Chelydra serpentina*), found nearly everywhere in the United States east of Colorado. Snappers are predators that hunt by burying themselves in the mud at the bottom of a sluggish stream or pond to wait for passing prey, which they capture in powerful jaws.

The survivalist walking along a stream bank should watch for a sudden cloud of silt at the bottom near the bank, created when a turtle withdraws beneath a cloud of muck. Probing the mud with a long stick can locate the turtle's hard carapace under the soft mud and help to lever it free from where it has dug in (snappers are surprisingly strong). This same probing method can be used in winter when turtles hibernate under mud close to shore in shallow water—in fact, hibernated turtles are safer to handle because they are too sluggish to bite.

The best way to handle any snapper is when it is dead, so take one only when you need meat. Their long snakelike necks—extendable to almost half their body length—have taken a few hunters by surprise, and a snapper's powerful beak can do considerable damage to flesh. The safest method is to push, prod, and shove

Snapping turtles are a valuable survival food across America, especially their eggs in early summer, but be afraid of the deceptively long neck and powerful jaws.

TURTLE TRACKS

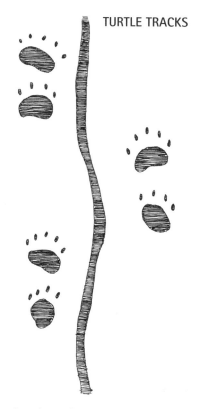

Snapping turtle tracks as they might appear in wet sand.

the turtle toward shore with a pair of long stout sticks. Once cornered onshore, incite the animal to bite a stick held in front of its nose (remember that long reach), and when the head lunges forward to grab, lop off the neck with your knife or crush it with a rock.

Cleaning a turtle is simple. The upper shell (carapace) and lower shell (plastron) can be separated by using a sharp knife to cut through the skin between the legs where the two shells join around their perimeters. Extend these cuts down each leg to the foot and peel the skin away, cutting both skin and feet free at the joint. The legs are the meatiest part of the turtle, followed by the back muscles. When the plastron and carapace have been separated, cut all four legs free and strip the meat from the spine with a small sharp knife. The meat should be washed thoroughly to help lessen the strong wild taste. The meat can be cooked on a spit or cut into small pieces and boiled with fern fiddleheads, burdock root, or rice.

Turtle eggs are available only in early summer–from the beginning of May to early June in most places. Snapping turtle eggs should never be passed up as survival food. During the laying period, female snappers can be seen excavating surprisingly deep nest chambers, usually along sandy shorelines. The determining factor for the location of a nest is water, because no turtle can travel far; even the rough cinders of abandoned railroad grades near waterways have been dug out by turtles to receive clutches of about forty eggs the size of a Ping-Pong ball. The marble-size eggs of smaller painted turtles that nest in the same environment are also edible, but more are needed for breakfast.

The best method of obtaining only fresh turtle eggs is to wait in early morning before the sun is up by shorelines where there has been obvious nesting activity: dug-up shorelines and especially the curled papery-looking shells of eggs that have already been pilfered by raccoons or even bears. There might be several territorial mothers on a shore, their grudges forgotten when egg laying starts. Wait for one to finish, then it will recover the nest with loose dirt; when the turtle leaves, carefully excavate the nest—usually to

Snapping turtle eggs

about ten inches—until you feel or see the leathery shells. The flexible shells are tougher than those of bird eggs, and they transport well in a bag, sock, or hat. Be aware that you are in competition with many species for these seasonal delicacies.

Except for a tougher shell that needs to be cut open, turtle eggs can be prepared every way a chicken egg can. You can boil them for five minutes, scramble them in a skillet, or cook them sunny side up on a flat rock over a fire. Yolks are proportionally large with less white than a chicken egg, and the cooked yolk is slightly coarser, but turtle eggs are as palatable and nutritious a survival food as you'll find anywhere.

Frogs

In North America all frogs are edible, although only the eight-inch bullfrog is large enough to be considered game. The muscular hind legs of smaller green and pickerel frogs, among others, are also edible, but more are required to make a meal.

Frogs can be gathered along a shaded stream bank with a heavy stick in hand. Those hiding in the grass will leap into the water at your approach, then typically stick their heads out of the water to look back at what it was that frightened them. A hard whack kills the curious amphibians instantly. This is also where your frog spearhead can come in handy.

Probably the most effective daylight way to gather frogs is the hook-and-line method. This frog-fishing technique uses a long slender pole to dangle an impaled fly or bee in front of the hungry frog. Fooled into thinking that it has an easy meal within reach, the frog lashes out with its long tongue and draws the bait into its mouth. Pull the hooked animal to shore and kill it with a sharp rap on the head.

Even the largest frog has little meat on its body aside from the hind legs. Remove these from the body of the dead animal by cutting each of them off at the pelvic joint, then remove the skin by peeling it backward toward the foot like a banana and cutting it off at the lowest joint. The peeled legs can then be cooked on a hot rock next to the fire or water fried in a mess kit skillet.

Although most species are small, the muscular hind legs of all frogs are edible, and most are easily gathered using only a stout club.

Birds

The best tool for obtaining fresh game, especially birds, in a real-life do-or-die situation is with a scoped .22 caliber rifle. Almost every bird is edible ("fish" birds like seagulls and mergansers are unpalatable), and some type of bird is nearly always abundant. Like chickens, the meatiest portions are always the breasts then the thighs. Some birds are larger than others, but a belly filled with the meat of a dozen sparrows is full just the same. As with any game, opportunistic hunting—taking game as you encounter it—is the most efficient method acquiring a meal. Unless you can make a head or neck shot (where you'll either kill the bird or miss it entirely), Canada geese are too large for even a hypervelocity .22 long rifle round like Remington's Yellowjacket, but mallard and

145

other ducks can be stopped with an expanding bullet through the wings or breast.

Waterfowl

When using any projectile weapon to take waterfowl, whether a rifle, slingshot, or bow and arrow, try to stalk the quarry from high ground overlooking the waterway. Ducks and geese have keen eyesight, but like most animals they tend not to look up for danger. A stealthy hunter can work himself into position for a clean shot on swimming waterfowl if he can remain above the birds as they swim past.

Waterfowl can be taken with a field-made bow and arrow. A hunter hidden in the brushy shoreline of a flocking hole, where waterfowl nest in summer and congregate during spring and autumn migrations, can often ambush passing birds at close range. Again, an elevated position is best, especially from within shadows—never underestimate a duck's eyesight, or its ability to detect the slightest movement.

Wild Turkey

Once decimated by overhunting, the American turkey is now found in rural and wilderness areas across the United States. American Indians hunted these big birds by simply following them and shooting them as the flock foraged for food. Turkeys can fly only a short distance, so those that fly away can be stalked again until you lose sight of it for good or clean it for dinner. Turkeys are not migratory and can be run down on foot by catching them on the ground after a deep snow that inhibits the big birds from spreading their wings. For that reason, turkeys are not found in thick swamps that would hamper take-off or in scrub forests that lack large trees with thick branches to roost on.

The best time to catch a sharp-eyed but night-blind turkey unaware is early nightfall, when whole flocks roost in large trees to avoid predators, their bodies silhouetted against a not quite dark sky. Roosting trees are marked by scats and plucked feathers on the ground below, and the same tree will probably be used indefinitely, so long as the local food supply holds out.

A head shot is the best bet for the turkey hunter armed with a .22 rifle; those using the bow and arrow should aim to pierce the body, then trail the wounded bird until it can be caught. Turkeys are gregarious and flocks are active from daylight to dusk. Turkey eggs can be found in large leafy nests on the ground from late April to early May and can be prepared like chicken eggs.

Grouse and Relatives

Grouse and quail are found across America, and despite differences in habitat, their behaviors are similar. During the spring mating season, males can be downright stupid, advertising themselves with calls ranging from the chainsawlike drumming of a ruffed grouse to the warbling, fluttering dance of a woodcock. In fact, some prime males might actually puff up at a human, which makes them easy prey.

Walk softly, and be ready to shoot; whether armed with a makeshift bow-and-arrow or a scoped .22 rifle, most of the game a survivor encounters will be opportunistic, so it pays to keep a weapon close to hand while hiking.

Like turkeys, these proportionally heavy-bodied birds are not usually long-distance fliers, and birds that are flushed can be stalked again. Most are reluctant to take flight, preferring to rely on camouflage, and prairie species tend to run from danger before flying from it.

Bird Foot Snare

In the survivalist's toolbox, the bird foot snare is like a screwdriver: simple but useful enough to be indispensable. This is another instance where only man-made nylon string will suffice, whether sixty-pound packaging string for turkeys and geese or twenty-pound fishing line for grouse, because no natural cordage is as slippery or as strong. This trap is much like the "drag" snares used by elephant poachers who catch their prey by one leg with a cable, but anchor the opposite end to a heavy log that is exhausting to drag yet can't be pulled against with the victim's full strength.

The concept of the foot snare is devilishly simple: A number of large nooses are arrayed around a central anchor point, which might be a heavy drag or a fixed stake, depending on circumstances and prey. Nooses should lie nearly flat, except one side should be slightly higher than the other to allow the bird's foot to slip under. If available, rice can be used to help attract feeding birds (one survivalist I know keeps a supply of bird seed for that reason). The next step with that leg pulls against the noose, causing it to tighten around the ankle, where the foot itself holds the snare from slipping free. Lacking an ability to understand their predicament, birds and most other animals will simply pull harder, tightening the noose even further. Some mammals that might fall into the trap have been known to escape by gnawing off a foot, so check your snares frequently.

When you see that a bird is caught by your snare, waste no time in dispatching it or it might become frantic enough to break free. Beware the bludgeoning wings of geese, the raking spurs of turkeys, and the sharp beaks of many birds. For larger birds, a stout club brought hard against head or neck is quick and sure. Smaller birds can be killed by twisting their necks hard several

FOOT SNARE FOR BIRDS

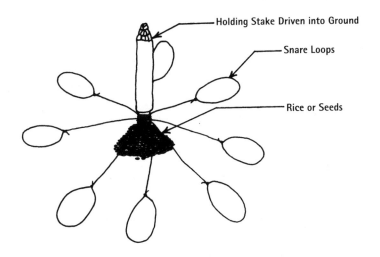

Holding Stake Driven into Ground

Snare Loops

Rice or Seeds

times. Chicken farmers simply yank a bird's head off completely, letting the decapitated chicken bleed out prior to cleaning.

Cleaning Birds

Preparing a bird for cooking is easy: Lop off the head, make an incision from the anus to the breastbone, and pull out the entrails; do not cut through the breastbone, as the edges can be very sharp. I don't recommend plucking the bird; skinning is easier, and bird skin rips using just the fingers. Larger tail and wing feathers will have to be pulled free, but skinning keeps the number of down feathers that go up your nose to a minimum. When skin and feathers are gone, wash the carcass, and you're ready for cooking.

Cooking Birds

The simplest method of cooking any bird is to skewer it through both wings on a green sapling, which is then suspended across a low fire by a crotched (Y-shaped) stake drilled into the earth on either side. More heat than flame, the cook fire should have a coal bed broad enough to surround the bird with radiated heat, fed only as many small pieces of wood as are necessary. Rotate the bird from time to time to ensure even cooking, and when the breast meat peels away cleanly from the bone, the bird is ready to eat.

If cookware (including cans found on the trail) is available, birds can be cut up and boiled until the meat literally falls from the bones. Cook bird carcasses with fiddleheads, burdock roots, or wild carrots, pick out the bones, and you have a wilderness chicken soup to rival grandma's.

Mammals

While few real-world survivors have the need to tan hides and fashion skin clothing, mammals can have great importance as food. Great variety exists in the needs and habits of individual species, but some characteristics are fairly generic. Most animals are territorial, staking off claimed areas with boundary markers of urine and scat. Most of them are crepuscular, or most active during the hours of dusk and dawn, when they travel between feeding areas and secluded sleeping places.

All animals tend to fall into routines and will travel the same routes twice a day unless disturbed. All animals can be counted on to be intimate with every feature of their domain and to avoid any foreign objects that suddenly appear. Trails are used by many species, and all of them have alternate branches that an animal can take if it perceives danger on the usual trail.

By knowing the animals we eat and their habits, it's possible to exploit the natural order of things to get a good meal of red meat. The following are hunting tips for taking some of the animals that are likely to serve as food in a survival situation.

Porcupines

In most of the United States and nearly all of Canada this easily recognized vegetarian (*Erethizon dorsatum*) is common and even a nuisance in some areas. Almost impervious to attack from any predator except man, it is one of the few species that can be outrun by a human. Most active during the summer months when they sleep the day away on lofty branches, descending at dusk to feed on ground plants, porcupines can often be caught on the ground in open places just before dark. For this prey, you need only a heavy green-cut club, four feet long by at least two inches at the butt.

The first thing a threatened porcupine will do is head for a tree to climb, but it will probably keep its behind toward you at all times, turning in the opposite direction when you place yourself in its path (porcupines have never been known to charge). The species' best defense is its spiny tail, which it swings like a club to leave natural predators with a face full of painful quills. With your club, you can safely herd and prod the animal to keep it from escaping overhead, and maneuver it into a killing position.

Porcupines are legendary for their ability to absorb a magazine of buckshot while continuing to climb a tree, but trauma to the brain kills the animals easily. A .22 bullet to the head is easiest, but a club-wielding survivalist can achieve an instant kill by bringing his bludgeon down hard across the bridge of a porcupine's nose, between its eyes.

Porcupines mate in November—the only time you'll see solitary adults together—and pregnant females winter in dens that range from rock crevices to standing hollow trees, both marked by accumulations of brown pellet-shaped feces at the base. Pellets average one inch in length and about three-eighths of an inch in diameter with a sawdustlike texture, and the darker the pellets, the more recent the scat. Fresh scats are a good sign, because porcupines do not migrate fast or far, and the den owner will probably be found within a one-hundred-yard radius.

In a snow-locked forest, porcupines may climb a large pine— especially white pines—and remain in its branches for several days, feeding on tender twigs, buds, and young bark. These feeding trees are easy to spot by the number of nipped-off pine sprigs lying around the base of the tree, and if those clippings are fresh, you can expect that the porcupine is still in the tree. With projectile weapons, any treed porcupine requires a killing head shot, because mortally wounded porkies are notorious for digging into tree bark with their large claws and hanging on for days after they die.

Rabbits and Hares

Rabbits and hares (lagomorphs) are a plentiful source of fresh meat throughout North America. All of them make their homes in swamps, sagebrush, or some other type of concealing vegetation; birthing dens are usually under brush piles, fallen logs, or in the abandoned dens of other animals.

All members of this species digest rough plant fibers through "fecal fermentation," meaning that they eat the same food twice, pooping out little green balls, about three-eighths of an inch in diameter, of half-digested plant matter. Left alone, a rabbit or hare

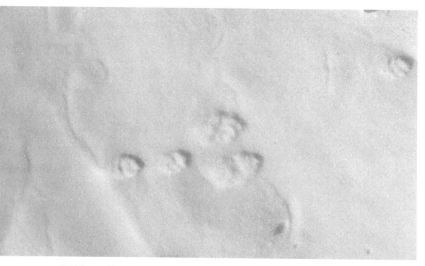

Rabbits and hares are the most prevalent game animals in almost every environment, and the Snowshoe Hare tracks shown here are typical of the track pattern of all species.

reingests the green spheres, finally expelling them as fully-digested balls of compressed brown plant fibers. A hunter who finds initial-stage green balls knows that the animal's feeding routine has just been interrupted, and that it is probably within a few yards and may return to finish if the intruder withdraws.

If you have a .22, the trick to getting a rabbit on the spit is to exploit its weaknesses: Rabbits and hares are fast short-distance sprinters that habitually flee to nearby cover, then freeze. They are also near-sighted, and sometimes when they freeze in a place where they can't see you, you can still see them—especially with a scoped rifle. Head shots are recommended, but rabbits and hares tend to go down easily with body shots. The same method works with shorter-range arrows and slingshots, but with greater difficulty because you need to get closer to the prey.

Bunnies are among the easiest animals to snare because there are usually a lot of them, and they move in a hopping motion that helps to jerk a snare noose tight. Once caught by the neck in a choker that only gets tighter as they pull, rabbits (and most animals) panic and struggle even harder until they expire from strangulation or a broken neck (see pp. 148, 149 on constructing snares).

Rabbits may travel the trails made by other species, but their own trails are too narrow and overgrown to accommodate larger species, which helps to narrow down the best locations for your snares. The point where a trail enters a brush pile or the hollow under a snow-covered dogwood is ideal for catching animals entering or exiting their refuge. In snow, the trenchlike packed trails that rabbits use throughout winter can be dotted with snares at each of their many intersections.

As always, set as many snares as you can to help ensure success—two rabbits are better than no rabbits. Check your snares every few hours, because a rabbit might run into your trap while fleeing a predator, and it is not uncommon to find a sprung snare with only the prey's head left in the noose. After retrieving caught rabbits, the snare can be reset, because lagomorphs are blessed with a short memory and limited intellect.

WILD TURKEY

Very large, standing three to four feet high. Roosts in trees and feeds on the ground. Diet consists of insects, berries, nuts, and seeds. Found in deciduous forests and wooded bottomlands. Nests on ground in spring.

CANADA GOOSE

Twenty-two to forty inches tall. Usually found near water, but may occasionally be found in corn or grain fields, especially in fall and spring. Nests on elevated ground near water in spring.

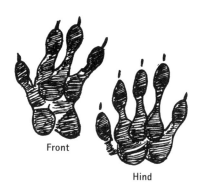

Front

Hind

WOODCHUCK OR GROUNDHOG

Fourteen to twenty inches long, excluding tail. Burrows underground. Hibernates in winter. Found in open forests, forest edges, and fields.

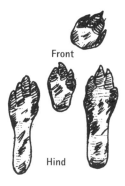

Front

Hind

SNOWSHOE JACKRABBIT

Fifteen to nineteen inches long. Brown in summer, coat turns white in winter. Active mostly at night but can often be found standing motionless in brush or deep grass during the day. Found nearly everywhere, but seems to prefer swamps and thick brushy areas. Toes can spread very wide in snow.

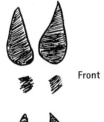

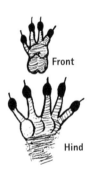

WHITETAIL DEER

Four to six feet long and up to four feet tall at shoulder, but usually less. Long tail white or underside, raises when alarmed. Active early morning, midday, and early to late evening. Feeds mainly at night in open fields and meadows. Beds down in swamps and other thick cover during the day. Eyesight poor, hearing and smell acute. "Yards up" in winter, feeding on cedars and marsh grass when normal feeding areas are covered with snow.

Front

Hind

SQUIRREL

Eight to eleven inches long, excluding tail. Found in oak, maple, and beach forests. Occasionally found in pines. Nests high in trees. Nests are leafy mass lodged in branches. Active all year but mostly in fall when nuts and acorns ripen.

Front

Hind

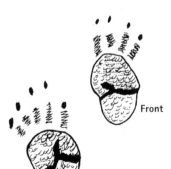

PORCUPINE

Eighteen to twenty-three inches long, excluding tail. Mostly nocturnal, and may often be seen sleeping high up in a tree. Can be found in brushy areas and forests, but seems to prefer pines. Active all year.

Note: Tracks shown are as they might appear in mud or soft earth. Perfect tracks, such as those shown, are more often the exception than the rule. Tracks in snow may look different.

Front

Hind

Squirrels

The squirrel family (*Sciuridae*) is diverse, encompassing red, gray, and fox tree squirrels but also burrowing woodchucks, chipmunks, and other ground squirrels. All are edible and palatable if cooked to tenderness. Except for flying squirrels, all of them are diurnal, or active during the day.

A common trait among all species is a roundish front track with four well-clawed toes, and an elongated hind track with five clawed toes, like rabbits and hares, except that most squirrels are smaller and live in different habitats. The usual gait is a hop, which often leaves sets of front and hind tracks that resemble the paired-exclamation-point (!!) pattern of rabbits and hares.

Burrowing squirrels are most easily taken by shooting them as they go about their daily business, always close to a burrow entrance. They are probably most easily caught by setting a snare

Red squirrels and chickarees are small, very territorial tree squirrels whose aggressive natures make them a prime target for a hungry survivor armed with a projectile weapon.

at each den entrance—there will be at least one back door—so that occupants have no choice except to pass through the noose (be aware that snaring burrow entrances is illegal in most states).

Traditional tree squirrel hunters often bag their limits by finding a forest with obvious squirrel activity—usually the animals themselves—then just sitting quietly against a comfortable tree.

Taking one will cause the woods to go silent for a few minutes, but if you continue to sit quietly, resident squirrels will resume their business as though you've been forgotten.

In conifer forests, especially, the most common squirrel will be the eastern red squirrel or the closely related western chickaree. Although these small squirrels are often hated for raiding bird feeders, their aggressive nature can make them easy targets for a traveling survivalist. I once lived on red squirrels for eight days during a real-life survival situation. Frequently the bold rodents reveal themselves by scolding intruders with loud chattering, and elevated feeding platforms scattered with peeled pine cones are a sure sign of red squirrels.

Raccoons

Raccoons (*Procyon lotor*) are common throughout the United States, Mexico, and southern Canada, and they can be a valuable food source under do-or-die conditions. With an omnivorous diet and few natural enemies, raccoons can survive in most environments but tend to gravitate toward water. They patrol shorelines at night for crayfish, clams, small fish, and almost any other small, tasty animal, leaving distinctive tracks in the wet sand or mud. A hidden hunter overlooking a likely shoreline may catch foraging raccoons by surprise. As a boy trapper, I took many raccoons while just walking quietly and slowly through hardwood forests where the animals denned and slept during the day.

Despite raccoons' cuteness, veteran hunters will attest to the ferocity of a cornered or wounded raccoon, so the best method of dispatching one is with a bullet through the brain pan. A sharp-tipped arrow through the body—don't count on an arrow to pierce the skull—is probably second best, but be prepared to follow up with two or three more shots. Those accustomed to housecat-size raccoons of the Southwest might wonder why the trepidation, but an encounter with an ornery sixty-pounder in the north woods is cause to fear for your safety.

Next up on the hard-core scale is killing a raccoon with a fish or frog spear. The trick is to charge from a hiding place toward a raccoon at the shoreline and to panic it into heading for deeper water. In one foot of water, the raccoon will need to start swimming. At this point, you can catch up to it, then plunge the barbed spearhead into its spinal area. This wound will not kill the animal; it only enables the raccoon to be handled at arm's length until it can be pinned to the ground and dispatched with a heavy club to the skull.

Raccoons may be hanged by a pencil snare (see pp. 174–77 for a description) placed across the trail from their bedding areas to a shoreline, but probably the most productive snare technique is to lay a dozen or so loose foot snares (described on pp. 148, 149) along the shoreline just into the water. Do not stake the loose end of the snare line but tie it to a dead branch or other drag that weighs around five pounds, then hide nearby because you'll need to move as soon as the screeching starts (maybe after dark), or your prey is sure to escape. The drag slows a panicked raccoon enough to be run down and bludgeoned to death with a long, heavy club—and to keep it from getting to you.

Some people have likened the taste of raccoon meat to lamb, and I can taste the similarities—I don't like either. Like bears, raccoons acquire a thick layer of fat in preparation for winter, and while the fat is less than tasty, it is rich and just what a hard-working survivor needs to stave off the same fat starvation that temporarily paralyzed the Lewis and Clark expedition with crippling diarrhea and cramps. Eating fat sounds gross to most people, but to a carnivore, fat is one of the most prized, and least available, high-energy foods; if your body wants it, so will your taste buds.

Beavers

The beaver (*Castor canadensis*) lives at the edge of flowing waters throughout North America and Canada and today is prevalent enough to be considered a pest by many owners of riverfront property. Strict vegetarians, these large (about twenty pounds for mature males) aquatic rodents are nature's lumberjacks, toppling and feeding on the bark and buds of birch and aspen trees but also river willows and ground plants. When waters freeze over, beavers may remain in their lodges or dens for weeks, living off the bark and twigs of tree branches they've anchored in the muddy bottom just outside. Lodges may be the classic dome-shape structures of sticks and mud, especially in places where a beaver family has created its own pond by damming a stream. In rivers that are always deep enough to permit an upward-sloping underwater entrance to the den, you'll find "bank beavers" that build neither dams nor lodges and whose presence may be revealed only by gnawed-down saplings, tracks in mud, or the animals themselves.

Generally regarded as nocturnal, beavers in a wilderness may be active any time of day. A hunter can prompt beaver activity by tearing a hole in the animals' dam (not an easy task), then hiding within shooting distance until the sound of escaping water brings them to plug the hole.

Head shots with a rifle are the order of the day because a dead beaver floats downstream to you, but a wounded beaver will dive and head for its lodge. Arrows should be barbed, fired from close range, and if possible, discharged where the beaver cannot easily escape—like the trickling cul-de-sac formed at the base of most dams. Be prepared to shoot a beaver several times with arrows, then dispatch it with a club to the head. Do not be tentative with this animal, and stay out of biting range at all costs.

Beavers are one of the easier animals to snare. They habitually use the same places to climb out of and slide into the water, and these "slides" are obvious foot-wide trails of pressed-down grasses at water's edge (otter slides are half as wide). A snare set across these pathways is likely to catch one of the colony by its neck. Likewise, a dozen foot snares can be arrayed on the ground in places of beaver activity and anchored to immovable points, but these should be watched closely to ensure that snared animals don't escape.

Beaver meat is very good, similar to rabbit, and the fatty tail is considered a delicacy among northern Indians. Before skinning, the very first thing to do is to cut off and discard the skunky-smelling perineal glands near the anus, then thoroughly clean your knife blade (or get a new sharpened rock). Musk from those glands is used by beavers as a territorial marker, and getting the oils onto exposed meat will make it unpalatable enough to induce gagging. (This same problem exists with the tarsal glands on the inside knee of white-tailed deer.)

Whitetail Deer

Whitetail deer (*Odocoileus virginianus*) and western mule deer (*Odocoileus hemionus*) are also on the survivalist's menu, but a yearling deer can produce forty pounds of boneless meat.

Processing that much will require staying in one location for two days while the meat dries in strips over a low fire to become about five pounds of jerked meat. Sporting sensibilities do not apply to survival, and, like natural predators, a person who needs to kill for food should target the weakest and most easily overcome individuals.

Deer are grazing herbivores that tend to be nocturnal, frequenting fields and meadows to feed on ground plants each evening, then returning to a secluded, usually swampy (with a source of drinking water), bedding area at dawn to sleep and chew their cud. They are very alert at this time and able to disappear in a single leap in most bedding places, so a survivalist's best bet is to ambush one of them as it travels a regular trail between feeding and sleeping spots at dawn and dusk. Regularly used trails will be obvious, with fresh, sharp-edged hoof prints in both directions. Do not disturb the trail, but hide yourself downwind and within shooting range, making as little impact on the area as possible. Do not construct a hunting blind, as this could cause every animal in the area to avoid you.

For political reasons, outdoor writers tend to ignore the fact that hypervelocity .22 rimfires like the CCI Stinger or Remington Yellowjacket have proved to be decisive deer killers at ranges up to one-hundred yards. Conservation officers report that poached deer taken with head shots by these bullets suffer massive trauma and usually instant death, with complete skull penetration to at least fifty yards. None of the rimfire cartridges has sufficient hydrostatic power to reliably take game larger than forty pounds with body shots; if you can't get a head shot, don't shoot.

Deer may be killed with an arrow, but even with modern broad-heads and bows, arrows are not often a fast killer of large game, mostly causing damage to internal organs after impact.

Preferred targets include all angles that will penetrate the prey's chest cavity (the heart sits low in the chest). Even if the deer falls immediately (unlikely), wait about ten minutes before approaching the carcass; spooking a deer that is not fully expired almost guarantees that it will flee in an adrenaline-induced panic. Mark carefully where a wounded deer flees (it will always head for thick brush to lie down), and when you finally go to retrieve it, follow its trail with all the stealth you can muster, with arrow nocked and ready to make a follow-up shot. Early Native Americans sometimes trailed the same deer for more than a day, shooting it several times before it could be eaten. Deer should be considered a last resort for the survival bow and arrow.

Deer are wary and equipped with senses we can only guess about; they can sometimes be snared in a head noose but show an uncanny knack for sidestepping snares suspended across their trails.

Better are foot snares of 550-pound parachute cord anchored to 100-pound drags that won't let a victim pull against them with full strength but seriously inhibits the animal's mobility while leaving a clear trail to wherever it goes.

Dispatching a crippled or caught deer can be dangerous because flailing hooves can strike with the force of hammers. If possible, the hunter's technique of pinning a deer to the ground by lying across its neck (as you would to control a horse), then driving a

Historically, hunters have not had a good track record when it comes to wilderness survival, but today an entire no-fail survival outfit can be fitted into a few pockets.

long-blade knife upward through the lower jaw and into the brain is a method that works for all animals. If the animal cannot be approached safely, use a long stout club to reach past its defenses with a hard felling blow to the head or neck, but be ready to follow up immediately with one or two killing blows across the skull.

Processing Game

Before any animal can be used as food it must first be skinned and gutted. The following method is simple and clean and works well with all four-footed animals, whatever their size or species.

Deer-size game should only be taken as a last resort in dire circumstances; if you deem it necessary, be prepared to stay in one place for about two days while you dry strips of meat into jerky over a low fire.

Since the porcupine is often the most likely animal to serve as survival fare, and because it's the most difficult animal to skin, we'll use it as an example.

With this method, called "tube-skinning" by furriers, the hide is removed from the animal in one piece without opening the stomach cavity, although severing belly skin from anus to neck makes it easier to peel off. Larger animals like deer or wild pigs are most easily skinned by first hanging them upside down by the hind legs from a tree limb. This will keep the hindquarters spread wide apart and allow one to pull hard while removing the hide.

The first step is to make a cut around the circumference of the lowest joint of both of the animal's hind legs. These cuts are then connected by another cut that runs along the inside of each leg and across the anus. Always keep a porcupine on its back whenever possible during skinning because most of its quills are concentrated on the tail and the back; the belly is covered with wiry hairs but not quills.

Next, strip the hide away from the hind legs and down toward the head as far as possible. Sever the tailbone with a twisting, pressing motion, but don't cut the tail free of the body. Grasp both hind feet, one in either hand, place the heel of one foot on top of the tail, and pull hard upward. With luck, the hide will peel down to the shoulders with a single stroke. If the tail pulls free of the body, just kick it aside and repeat the procedure by placing a heel

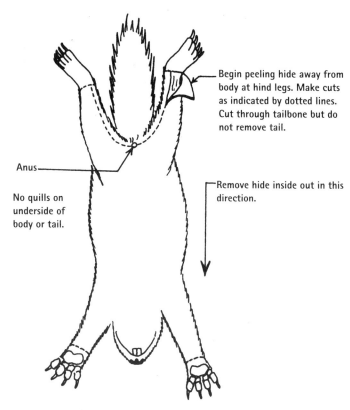

Begin peeling hide away from body at hind legs. Make cuts as indicated by dotted lines. Cut through tailbone but do not remove tail.

Anus

No quills on underside of body or tail.

Remove hide inside out in this direction.

GENERIC TUBE-SKINNING METHOD

on the freshly loosened skin and pulling again. When the hide has been peeled inside out down to the shoulders, free the front legs down to the paws and cut them free. Sever the neck in the same manner. The head and forepaws will remain attached to the hide, leaving you with a skinless carcass.

The last step is to remove the hind feet and eviscerate the animal. Remove the entrails by making an incision from the anus through the rib bones and down to the neck. This incision is best made by inserting the blade of the knife, cutting edge up, under the belly muscle and simply sliding it along. Cutting from the inside out in this way will lessen the chance of puncturing the stomach, the contents of which emit such a strong odor that the uninitiated have been known to vomit. Split the pelvic bone by driving the blade through the anal canal.

When the stomach cavity has been opened from the anus to the neck, remove the entrails by pulling downward and outward from the chest cavity, not on the organs themselves but rather on the membrane they're attached to. A knife will help to separate this thin, tough membrane from the ribs, taking all the innards with it.

If water is available, wash the cleaned carcass thoroughly and remove any pieces of organs that might still be attached, especially in the neck and the anal canal. If the stomach or other internal organs were punctured during cleaning, be sure to remove any of their contents from the meat, as well as any blood clots, and cut away any darkened, bruised portions; all of these will impart an unpleasant taste to the meat.

Cooking Game

No need to be fancy when butchering an animal in the wild. A noticeable line of white fat marks where major muscle groups meet at the front and back of all four legs and also marks the location of leg bones. Cut along the white line down to the bone on both sides. Cut the chunks of meat loose at either end and work them free from the bone with your knife tip. Slice out the tenderloin muscles that parallel the spine, and generally remove as much meat from bones as possible. Cut large pieces of meat into narrow strips that dry quickly when suspended over a low fire or placed next to it while draped across a stone or log. Once jerked, the meat can remain edible for months carried in a cloth bag that breathes.

Campfire recipes vary with the availability of other complementary foods. The simplest method of cooking small game is to roast the entire carcass on a spit over a low fire. If you have a cooking vessel, the addition of a few cattail shoots, wild carrots, leeks, burdock root, watercress, and other wild vegetables can produce a nutritious, palatable soup. The same dish can be prepared using meat from fish, fowl, reptiles, or even insects.

Snakes

All snakes are edible, although some are too small to be considered as a survival food. Snakes are cold-blooded creatures that become dormant in temperatures below fifty degrees Fahrenheit (cold-tolerant garter snakes are an exception). In snow country they hibernate through the winter months, sometimes in colonies, and emerge again when temperatures rise in spring. They sun themselves on rocks and other open areas in the morning before the night chill has disappeared. In the heat of the day they take refuge under logs and rocks, and some desert snakes, like the sidewinder, bury themselves in the sand. Snakes seek refuge in the same places to escape the cooling effects of rain. Where temperatures remain warm through the night, many species are active from dusk until dawn. All snakes are predators, and since most animals tend to gravitate toward water, shorelines are among the best places to hunt them.

Few snakes are venomous but nearly all will bite defensively, and some have enough teeth to draw blood. With this in mind, a snake hunter should be armed with a stout pole at least five feet in length. It need not be forked at the end, because the objective isn't to pin the snake, but to kill it with a hard blow to the head.

Cleaning a snake is simple. Carefully remove the head and discard it, because even dead snakes have been known to bite reflexively. With the head tossed well out of reach, make an incision in the belly from the anus to the point where the head was taken off. Beginning at the top, use a finger to strip out the entrails; they should come out in one piece.

Next, find a loose corner of skin where the head was removed and work it free until the skin can be grasped firmly between the thumb and forefinger. The skin can then be stripped downward in one piece. Wash the carcass thoroughly if sufficient fresh water is available.

Snake meat can be spitted and cooked over a low, open fire by weaving the spit in and out of the body to hold it securely, and turning as needed. It can also be boiled and included in a dish of wild vegetables, or if the animal is large enough, it may be sliced into tasty steaks.

Common to waters across the U.S., the sharp-toothed but non-venomous watersnake's territorial aggressiveness and large size make it easy prey for a hungry survivor armed with a club.

Insects

When I teach a survival course, I count on eating at least one insect to demonstrate that six-legged animals are food. Grasshoppers and crickets, ants, bees and wasps (with stingers cut off), moths, and fat white june bug larvae that evoke particularly strong reactions are all eaten by me as we find them. Most clients decline to eat an insect themselves, but I am obligated as a survival instructor to introduce them to the most abundant source of food on the planet.

The squeamishness humans feel about eating animals that are nutritious, often palatable, and in fact good food can be attributed to society not nature. Throughout history and around the world, insects have periodically played a critical role in human survival; a common response to locust swarms that stripped crops was to dry or smoke and then eat the insects, maybe until next year's crop was in. Scientists claim that pound for pound, grasshoppers—to name just one example—have more digestible proteins than beef. Grubs, maggots, and other insect larvae (some caterpillars are bitter or toxic) carry within their bodies the vital fats needed to sustain them during transformation to adults, or to fend off fat starvation in people who eat them. That so many humans have starved in places teeming with the nutrition their bodies needed to live is nothing less than tragic.

Although I break this rule myself, it's always a good idea to cook or dry insects on a fire before eating them, because some may be host to parasites that can infest humans. Heat, smoke, and dehydration kill the parasites and give some insects a crunchy texture and better flavor. Grubs boiled in water become solid inside—something like boiling an egg—and have a somewhat nutty taste.

Black ants were referred to as "sugar ants" by early Americans who roasted whole colonies in rawhide or burlap bowls over a low fire, then crushed the dried bodies to a powder known as "black sugar." Even in winter, lethargic colonies can be found inside rotting logs and stumps, and these tiny, high-energy morsels can have extraordinary nutritional value when every calorie is needed.

Red, or formica, ants are also edible, but the formic acid that gives them their name is bitter to the palate. However, red ants are very aggressive; knock off the top of a colony's hill, insert a foreign object, then bite off the soldier ants clinging to it. Ant eggs are also nutritious, but they are not abundant.

Bow and Arrow

The most complex—and effective—of primitive hunting weapons, the bow and arrow has a counterpart in every aboriginal culture. With a good one, a hunter can reach out to strike an accurate, lethal blow from many yards distant, something no other predator can do. Even so, field-expedient survival bows and arrows are not comparable to modern hunting equipment; it is best to restrict your shots to close range and to prey no larger than a raccoon, and always be ready to shoot a second, even third, arrow. Modern archers can rightfully expect to score quick, accurate kills on game out to and beyond fifty yards, whereas the most skilled Indian bowhunter of old knew that he would have to take his shot at no more than fifty feet and then trail the animal until it bled to death. Still, the primitive bow and arrow is better than a spear or club, and easier to master than a slingshot.

Staves for a survival bow can be whittled and painstakingly dried and formed, but what a person needs right off the bat is a weapon that can propel a projectile with lethal force into the vital organs of another creature. Many a youngster has proved that even a simple willow branch with a shoelace tied to the ends and sharpened unfletched sticks for arrows can take a gray squirrel off a tree branch if you shoot at it enough times. Likely bow staves are straight, six feet long, at least one-inch in diameter, and close to the same diameter at either end. Saplings of cedar, willow, ash, even maple, are good candidates but not pine, which tends to break when flexed. Don't worry if you can't find a perfectly straight stave, because natural bends can be used to determine the direction in which it will best flex.

As with the fishing bow (described on pp. 135–37), natural bowstrings are poor in comparison to modern cordage; woven plant fibers aren't very strong, and rawhide—if you can get it—stretches and rots quickly unless kept well greased (or waxed). Laces and drawstrings from clothing can be used, but the smart money is on someone who has several yards of cord stashed in a pocket. Whittle a shallow groove around the circumference of the bow stave at either end, about two inches from the butt.

Tie a double half hitch slipknot—like the one used for snare nooses—to one end of the bowstring, and slip the noose over the stave end into the notch. Tighten the noose hard to settle it into the groove, and lock the noose in place with two choker hitches.

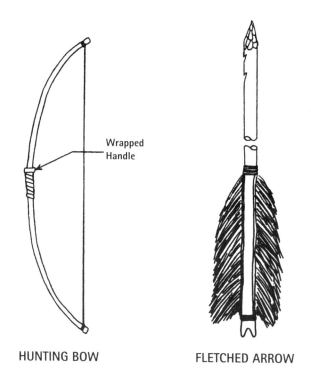

Wrapped Handle

HUNTING BOW   **FLETCHED ARROW**

Next, arch the bow stave by placing the tied end on the ground against the outside of one foot and bending the nontied end over the back of the opposite thigh. When the stave is flexed, pull the string taut against the nontied end with your free hand and adjust the amount of flex until there is about eight inches of space between the string and the center point of the stave (the point of its deepest bend). Wrap the free end of the string around the groove at the nontied end at least twice, and tie it off with choker hitches. The strung bow is now about five feet long and should have sufficient flex to permit a conventional full draw with roughly twenty pounds of force—more than sufficient for small game.

Draw the bow carefully a few times to be certain that the string is securely attached and that the stave won't break under pressure. A comfortable handle and arrow rest can be fashioned by wrapping several turns of cord (or safety tape) around the center of the bow.

Making Arrows

Workable arrows can be made from straight green seedling trees of most species, with suitable candidates being about three feet long and a half inch in diameter. Just whittling the narrowest end to a sharp point is sufficient to penetrate the body of squirrel-size animals, but hardness and penetration are maximized by charring shaped arrow tips in fire. Carefully cut a notch crosswise in the opposite thickest end of the arrow shaft to form a nock that accepts the bowstring.

Unfletched arrows fly straight enough to hit small targets thirty feet distant—far enough to take most small game—but real accuracy requires fletching the nock end of the arrow with split wing or tail feathers of almost any larger bird. Loose feathers can often be found along shorelines or under roosting trees. Split each feather lengthwise to create two fletching feathers that are, preferably, at least three inches long to provide the drag needed to keep any missile stable in flight.

Fletching feathers are positioned equidistantly around the shaft, about two inches from the nock, and with one feather always perpendicular to the nock to ensure that feathers make minimal contact with the bow when shot and do not deflect the arrow on release. Feathers are attached first by coating the mounting areas with pine pitch (commonly found exuding from minor wounds in pine trees) or another sticky sap. Dried pitch can be melted like hot glue, rehardening after it cools, but fresh sap may require a day or more to dry thoroughly. The ends of the fletching arrows must be secured by several turns of light thread from a sewing kit or unraveled from clothing or larger cordage or with braided fishing line, then glued in place with more pine sap.

Arrowheads

Arrowheads are not necessary for hunting small game—even if it doesn't penetrate, an arrow that hits a squirrel at more than a hundred feet per second can do crippling damage. If you deem them necessary, arrowheads can be fashioned by smashing bones that you find, then scraping and grinding (against a convenient rock) the shards to the desired spear shape. Knapped stone arrowheads can be works of art, but beginners will probably find it easy to knock functional arrowheads from available stones just by whacking them hard (and cautiously) against one another.

When an acceptable shard chips off—typically an elongated, sharply-pointed triangle at least two inches long and about a quarter inch thick—insert the narrow side of the triangle into the split end of an arrow tip to a depth of about one inch. Wrap the bottom of the split with several turns of light line to squeeze the two sides together, and fasten the head to the shaft with several X wraps that run from one side of the head around the shaft at its base and diagonally across the opposite side. It is not critical that an arrowhead be secured more than is necessary to hold it steady until it hits its victim; a point that breaks off in its victim is still lethal.

Archery

Archers learn to grip the bow's handle and rest the nocked (strung) arrow on the same side of the bow as the arm holding it (usually left, for right-handed people). The opposite hand hooks the string with the first joints of three fingers, pinning the nock between the index and middle fingers.

With the bow pointed upward at about forty-five degrees, lock the elbow of the arm holding the stave and bring the arrow down onto your target while drawing the arrow and string rearward; at full draw, the knuckle of your index finger should be just under your cheekbone. As gently as you can, release the string when you think your arrow is on target.

Beyond that, it pays to devote a little time to practice. Beginners generally achieve functional accuracy after a few shots, but modern bowhunters can be frustrated by bow staves that aren't perfectly straight and arrows that might not have exactly the same trajectory. Like an aborigine, a survivalist who was stuck long term would shave and whittle an archery outfit into a personally fitted work of art—and learn to compensate for idiosyncrasies. But the rough version described here is adequate for hunting small game and roosted birds, and it takes only a few minutes to become a hunter to be reckoned with.

Snares

Strangling snares are an icon of wilderness survival. Unlike foot or drag snares, which slow or hold an animal in place until it is dispatched, strangling snares are intended to be immediately fatal to their victims. The basic theory is that an unsuspecting game animal walks into an unseen noose that has been set to permit the animal's head to pass through but not its chest and shoulders. As the prey continues forward, its chest pushes against the loop's bottom, causing the noose to tighten from a slipknot at its top. When it does, the panicked animal will likely break into an instinctive run to escape, which only causes the noose to constrict even tighter. With no frame of reference from nature, and without the problem-solving intellect required to escape, most animals can only react in fight-or-flight mode, lunging madly against the anchored noose until they break their own necks or die of asphyxiation.

There are essentially two categories of strangling snare: spring snares and simple snares. True to its name, the simple snare is a loop of line, sometimes rope or wire, tied in a loose slipknot. The slipknot slides freely until the noose is pulled taut, then tightens against itself to help lock the noose around its victim's windpipe. Even cotton string has been used to catch rabbits, but occasionally a snared animal will chew through cord; some trappers remedy that problem by using light steel cable (fishing leader).

Spring snares release a restrained force to violently yank the noose tight around the victim's neck, even lifting it off the ground or decapitating large animals, depending on the spring force and the type of snare cord used. By providing their own killing force, instead of relying on an animal's struggles to kill itself, spring snares are decidedly lethal.

The weakest link in every spring snare is its trigger, the mechanism responsible for releasing pent-up spring force when tripped by a gentler outside force. Ideally, the trigger restrains a force sufficient to guarantee a quick death, yet releases that force with only a light pull, while remaining impervious to the elements (wind, ice, etc.) that could cause it to hang up, come loose prematurely, or otherwise fail. There are many designs for snare triggers, but I teach only one to my survival students

Pencil Snare

In terms of simplicity, reliability, and effectiveness, the pencil snare is probably the best survival snare for every environment. With two release points, or sears, the pencil snare is twice as likely to trip but is stable enough to resist the forces of wind and rain. It can be constructed from any environment that supports woody growth, and the design works well on every size of game.

With a little creativity, the pencil trigger can be employed for a variety of "sets" (traps), including trip wires, deadfalls, and even booby traps.

The components of a pencil snare are simple and easy to construct using only a knife; they consist of the snare cord, two notched anchor stakes, and the "pencil" trigger that fits into and is restrained by the notches in the anchor stakes. Wooden components are best made from dead wood that is dry but still firm enough to whittle; green wood is more difficult to shape. The size of the snare and its parts are dictated by the size of the animal it is intended to capture, but generally the anchor stakes are at least two inches in diameter, or at least twice the size of the pencil.

When cutting notches, first observe the classic rule of cutting away from yourself. With the knife in your preferred hand, press the cutting edge into the wood by pushing against the blade's unsharpened spine with the opposite thumb. For anchor stakes, use this method to shave thin layers that extend progressively deeper into the wood, each shaving extending an equal distance.

Every three or four layers, place the cutting edge across the top of the shavings, and press downward hard with a rocking motion that cuts the shavings free and leaves a flat bearing surface to better hold the pencil in place. Continue shaving and cutting (don't try to take too much wood at once) until the anchor notches are at least one-half inch deep and clean and flat at their top.

The pencil dictates how far apart the anchor stakes will be set and, in general, too wide is better than too narrow. The wood for the pencil should be straight and even and stout enough to restrain the amount of spring force being used. Gently shave the upper ends to give them a flat surface that mates well with the anchor stake notches.

The best snare cord is man made. Rawhide and braided plant fibers cannot match nylon cord for strength and toughness or for the slipperiness that is critical to smooth, fast noose operation.

Tensile strength, noose diameters, and snare heights should be matched to the weight of the animal being snared. For smaller game, ten feet per snare is more than sufficient.

With notched anchor stakes, pencil, and cord in hand, first make a noose from a loop of cord of the desired diameter—about eight inches for most small animals. Next, using the pencil length to determine how far apart to place the anchor stakes, drill the sharpened stakes into the soil in unobtrusive spots at either side of a likely animal trail; drilling them with a hard, twisting motion is most effective.

In most soils, with most game, stakes are anchored well enough at three inches. In snow, anchor stakes for snares and fishing sets are held in place by packing snow around their base then pouring a little water on the mounded snow to lock the stakes in ice.

Next, with the noose held open to the desired diameter, tie the cord, just above the slipknot, to the pencil's center. Wrap the cord around the pencil twice and tie it off with a square knot—the type of knot used isn't important, except that it has to be able to restrain a strong pull from above without pulling against the noose suspended from the pencil's underside. Set the pencil into the anchor stake notches to see how everything fits, and make adjustments as needed (noose diameter and height, stake height, notch angles, etc.).

When everything fits, all that remains is to "cock" the trap by connecting it to a lethal force, usually in the form of a green sap-

By increasing or decreasing the overall size of the pencil snare, it can be tailored to take animals from small to large.

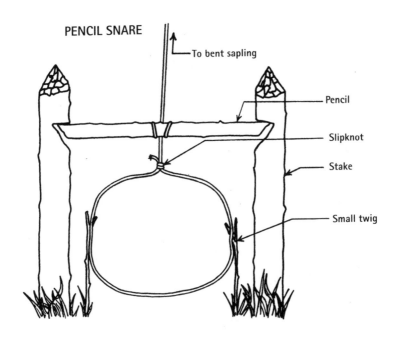

PENCIL SNARE

To bent sapling

Pencil

Slipknot

Stake

Small twig

ling at the side of an animal trail or a live branch overhead. If no suitable spring is available at the desired location, one can be created by drilling a long, stout sapling into the ground. Again, there is no need for complexity; the spring (sapling) only needs to be capable of exerting a strong upward pull against the pencil when the sapling is bent over and held under tension by the pencil in the anchor stake notches. When everything is cocked and in place, spread the noose to hold it open by hooking either side over blades of grass or tiny twigs. The noose's bottom should be suspended at least two inches above ground, to ensure that an animal passing in either direction will push against it with its legs or chest when its head passes through the noose.

Snare Placement

Snares are not as productive in the real world as movie writers might have us believe. Every fur trapper of old knew that the prey, whatever its species, would be intimately familiar with every stick and stone in its domain and would probably avoid any noticeable changes made to a regularly used trail. Keep that in mind when selecting a location for snares; if possible, use a snare cord that does not contrast with the surrounding terrain, and make as few changes to the environment as possible.

Game trails are the most likely places to set snares. Try not to leave your scent in the area (minimize movements, wear gloves if possible, etc.) or to leave obvious sign, but the best plan is to set as many snares as you can before nightfall, then "run" them in the morning to retrieve caught animals. If the snare is empty, reset it, and—survival strategy permitting—check them all again the next morning.

When making any survival tool, no technique is written in stone, and imagination is a powerful design tool. Available materials can be very different from one environment to another, or from season to season, and there is no right or wrong way to do anything; there are only methods that do or do not work. Practice the skills described here to understand their workings and to get tactile experience, but do not be befuddled if an environment doesn't provide precisely the materials you've been practicing with. For humans, fight or flight is a useless instinct; our adaptability relies on abstract thought and an ability to combine dissimilar products into the assembly of complex machines that make life easier. You belong to the most successful species on this planet, and if any animal can figure out how to stay alive, you can.

SIX
Orienteering

Most animals are born with an onboard organic compass. A ferric (magnetic) deposit at the tip of their nose is attached to neural connections that enable the animal's brain to "feel" the pull of earth's magnetic north pole. We also have a ferric deposit at the tip of our nose, but the sensory conduits between nose and brain are

Select a map that suits the terrain you'll be visiting: In the high Rockies, a topographical map that shows elevation and terrain contours is indispensable for identifying surrounding peaks; in the flat swamplands of Michigan's Upper Peninsula, where visibility is limited to yards, you need a detailed trail map.

not connected, and it has been proved time and again—sometimes tragically—that humans do not possess a natural sense of direction. This fact may be unacceptable to some people until they really get lost, but those who survive the experience will probably never again enter a woods without having at least one compass. (I carry two: a small one on a lanyard around my neck, and a fully loaded sighting compass in the map pouch clipped to my belt). To help mute the pain of knowing we are always one turn from being lost, this chapter also includes a few handy tricks for determining direction using visual clues from the environment.

Using the Compass

A number of survival students have been almost disappointed to find that basic orienteering with map and compass can be learned in a matter of minutes. All any compass really does is point to the planet's magnetic north pole when it is held flat in the palm, parallel to the ground. Rotating the compass so that its north indicator—and you—are facing north means east is directly to your right, south is behind you, and due west is left. Like every circle, there are 360 degrees around a compass dial. North is located at 360 degrees, which is also zero degrees, and progresses clockwise around the bezel to east (90 degrees), south (180 degrees), west (270 degrees), and back to north. The four directions (creating the acronym NEWS) divide a compass dial into equal fourths with 90 degrees between each quadrant. The opposite direction, or back azimuth, from any point on the compass dial is 180 degrees away in either direction. If the forward azimuth, or bearing, is 30 degrees (less than 180), add 180 degrees to arrive at a back bearing (reverse direction) of 210 degrees; if the forward bearing is 240 degrees (more than 180), subtract 180 degrees to get a back azimuth of 60 degrees.

For an average sport hunter or backcountry hiker, all that matters is that a compass keeps the individual on a straight course. Precise bearing numbers are important in more advanced orienteering techniques, but there are few places on earth where a person can be more than a day's trek from a marked trail or road—providing he or she knows which direction leads to that trail and can follow a straight line.

The beauty of a compass, as opposed to the technology-dependent GPS, has always been its simplicity and almost absolute reliability. It points toward magnetic north all the time, without batteries or parts that need replacing, it doesn't wear out or rely on satellites, and good ones are at least tough enough for serious field use. Potential problems are avoidable—like the need be sure your compass is not being influenced by nearby metal, whether from a Medic-Alert bracelet or a lightning-magnetized iron ore deposit. Some low-cost compasses can show a tendency to stick, especially in subzero weather (the liquid doesn't freeze, but movements can become tight). Large bubbles in liquid-filled compasses can also be trouble with pointer-type indicators (rotating dials are unaffected) because they can trap the indicator, and keep it from pointing to north. Always check that your compass is operating smoothly and normally by rotating your body back and forth a couple of times prior to taking a bearing. Never attempt to take a bearing within fifteen feet of a vehicle, or any large metal objects.

Just knowing where the four directions lie is enough to keep virtually anyone from making the very common mistake of wandering in circles, and if you can walk in a relatively straight line, few places on earth are more than a day's walk from the nearest road. But if you want to use your compass to get back out of the woods in a place close to where you came in, you'll need to take a bearing before you start. That means aligning your compass with north as described above, then using the information it provides to determine which direction you'll be taking into—and back out of—the forest.

For example, if you're about to enter a thick swamp from a two-track road, you need to know in which direction that road lies once it and other identifiable landmarks are out of sight. Landmarks like roads, trails, railroad grades, and power lines are the best targets for a back bearing (the direction that leads out) because they span large areas and are difficult to miss. If you leave the road and walk eastward into a woods, then finding that road again is as simple as walking west until you hit it. For most outdoor activities, that's all the orienteering you'll need to know.

Likewise, day activities like hunting and backcountry fishing may not need the complexity of precision instruments that are equipped with sights, map scales, clinometers, and other advanced orienteering tools. These compasses are designed to navigate accurately through any untracked wilderness in the world, but fully exploiting their potential demands more advanced orienteering techniques than are generally needed for getting to and from a camp or deer blind. The keystone of any orienteering outfit begins with a simple pocket compass worn around the neck on a lanyard and never taken off so long as you are in the woods.

A candidate for a pocket compass should be liquid filled to help its indicator settle quickly, with a movement that turns smoothly

THE COMPASS DIAL

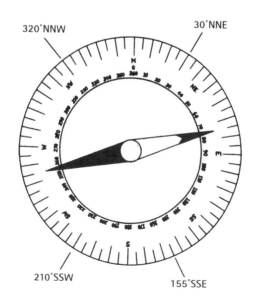

320°NNW

30°NNE

210°SSW

155°SSE

without sticking or jerking. Don't get the idea that simple has to mean low quality, however, because a good pocket compass is as serious an orienteering tool as its more sophisticated counterparts; it just lacks the precision sights and other accessories that most day hikers seldom need.

Magnetic Declination

Earth's true North Pole and its magnetic north pole are not in the same place. In North America there is only one longitude, which extends irregularly through Michigan to Florida, where both poles are in line with one another relative to the viewer. On either side of this North American "zero line," the two poles grow increasingly out of line with one another the farther one travels east or west.

MAGNETIC DECLINATION MAP OF THE UNITED STATES

Add the number of degrees indicated on the map to your compass reading if you are east of the zero declination line.
Subtract if you are west of the zero declination line.

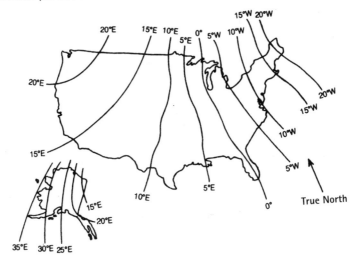

Confusion occurs because the standard reference point for maps is true north, which at some longitudes can be in a much different direction than the one your compass is pointing to.

In most places, with no more than a few miles from one large landmark to the next, declination (error) differences of a half dozen degrees are minor enough to be ignored. Ignoring a three-degree declination, for instance, will result in being off course by only about four hundred yards at the end of five miles. In places like the Alaskan coast, however, declination may be more than thirty degrees, and that is too large a discrepancy to ignore.

Correcting for declination is simple: Determine as closely as you can your actual position on a declination map, which shows in degrees how much difference there is between the two poles. If you are west (left) of the zero declination line, subtract the number of degrees indicated from every compass bearing; if your location is east (right) of the zero line, add the number of degrees indicated. Some orienteering maps are declination corrected, printed with longitudinal lines oriented toward magnetic north instead of true north—be sure you know which, because doubling the declination correction is bad too.

Map

Even the most basic orienteering outfit includes a map of the area being visited. This often underrated piece of equipment—which Lewis and Clark would probably have sacrificed organs to own—is vital to accurate navigation, and especially for plotting a route through terrain you haven't seen yet. One survival instructor in the Rockies claims that if he had to choose one he would take a map over a compass, because a map shows what lies all around and provides reference points from identifiable landmarks. In a deep lowland forest where visibility might be limited to a few yards and even mountains cannot be seen before you reach their base, you need both map and compass to first find, then identify, navigational landmarks.

For most outings, a simple trail map from a state's natural resources agency is more than adequate to keep you on a trail whose name you know or for determining where you are on a river. Off-trail and multiday adventurers, especially in mountain country, might opt for a more detailed topographical map that depicts changes in elevation with parallel (ridges) or concentric (mountains) lines that represent a drop or rise of (usually) ten feet. Whatever the terrain, a good map can help you avoid obstacles like canyons or swamps well before you encounter them, and if you can positively identify just one of the landmarks shown on your map, you cannot be lost.

Be sure that you know whether your map is declination corrected, because adding or subtracting declination twice is worse than ignoring it altogether. And based on one unfortunate personal experience, it is critical to protect your map from the elements

A sighting compass can serve as a simple compass and also take precise bearings to distant landmarks.

because losing your map can literally leave you lost. Maps printed on vinyl may be available for some areas, or you can laminate your own using clear adhesive contact (shelf) paper, available at most department stores.

GPS

What a compass cannot do is tell you exactly where you are. In dense forest where visibility may be limited to only a few yards, even the most sophisticated sighting compass is reduced to merely pointing toward magnetic north. That isn't a problem if you know where you came from and you've kept track of your route, but if you've just survived a plane crash in timber country, or had your kayak blown ashore by a typhoon, you might have only a vague idea of your location.

A GPS receives its coordinate data from geostationary satellites that serve as permanent electronic landmarks. By vectoring microwave signals from these fixed overhead beacons, a GPS can calculate its own location to within a few feet from anywhere under that umbrella of coverage.

In real life, heavy forest canopy has been known to block signals and prevent the unit from getting a satellite lock (connection), and so can falling snow or hard rain.

Subfreezing cold is tough on electronics; even with fresh batteries, a few hours of exposure to cold temps can lower voltage below the required operating threshold. Another problem is frosting of battery contacts, which is remedied by removing the cover and rolling batteries back and forth under your thumb a few times. Electronics are tolerant of heat up to about 160 degrees Fahrenheit, but temperatures of minus four Fahrenheit can destroy a unit's LCD screen, even crack its circuit board. The best safeguard against cold is to carry the unit in an inside pocket, keeping it as warm as possible.

A handy but potentially hazardous feature of a GPS is its "trek" or "plotter" mode. This function allows a person to wander without paying attention to landmarks or navigation while the GPS keeps track of directions and distances traveled. The user who wants to return sets the unit to its "backtrack" mode and simply follows an arrow displayed on the LCD. This is a useful feature, presuming the GPS remains operational. The danger comes from complacency, because using the plotter mode induces hikers to pay less attention to landmarks and direction. Should the unit be taken out of service, its user is likely to be completely lost.

Be aware that the map grids used to reference GPS and compass readings are very different from one another. The compass references are from a geometric scale that divides planet Earth into four equal parts of ninety degrees each, with zero degrees occurring at the International Date Line in Greenwich, England, for longitude (east–west) and at the equator for latitude (north–south). The large irregular squares formed by intersecting lines of latitude and longitude are subdivided into minutes (one-sixtieth of a degree) and seconds (one-sixtieth of a minute).

A GPS uses a system of sixty north-south grid zones and sixty east-west central meridian lines that begin and end at the same zero points in Greenwich and at the equator. Instead of breaking coordinates down into degrees, minutes, and seconds, the Universal Transverse Mercator grid uses a simpler base-ten system of meters. Depending on how close up the scale, or relief, is on your map, determining an exact position can be precise to within forty inches.

The bottom line is that the GPS and compass are valuable to a fully outfitted orienteer. A compass virtually guarantees that you will never be lost, but nothing beats a GPS for finding a remote cabin in untracked winter woods. Maybe the best advice is found on the first page of the instruction manual for Eagle Electronics' Expedition II GPS: "A careful navigator never relies on only one method to obtain position information."

Natural Compasses

Our species might have been denied the senses and bodies that allow "lower" animals to survive where a naked human would die, but our ability to understand and exploit an environment is unmatched. Where we lack a neurological sense of direction, we have an understanding that some things follow an order that is regular and predictable. Not being able to feel direction, we observe the reactions of other elements that respond predictably to forces from a regular direction.

The best known of these natural compasses is the sun, which all children learn will rise in the east and set in the west for every day of their life. Less known is that the Earth's moon follows the same east-west trajectory across the night sky. More importantly, always remember that our sun is directly overhead only at the planet's equator; the farther north one travels, the lower and more southerly the sun is in the sky. Face the sun at any time of day in Ontario, Canada, and you will be facing in a southerly direction (the opposite is true south of the equator).

In northern and high alpine forests where viciously cold northwesters are just part of winter, observers will note that the tops of the tallest conifers are mostly or completely devoid of branches on the north side. The most live branches will be growing from the top's southeast side, where they can serve as a valuable reference in deep forest where the sun might not be visible except at high noon.

Moss does not grow on the north side of trees; I mention this unkillable myth because to rely on it as true all the time could make a rough situation worse. In fact, in mature northern hardwoods where only the strongest trees have survived to cover the sky with a canopy, north winds can rip through the widely spaced trunks causing enough chill to prevent moss from growing except on the protected south side.

Stars have been reliable navigational beacons since the first hominid noticed that they were in the same place each night. Fortunately for me, you don't need to have an astronomer's knowledge of constellations to use them for navigation; you just need an open view to a clear night sky and an ability to recognize a few that are most visible. Orion's Belt, a diagonal of three stars running

A day hiking survival kit need not be cumbersome to ensure that its owner will live through a disaster, but it must be effective (one of these hikers is diabetic), and the kits of several hikers together should complement one another to form a more comprehensive survival system than any one of them carries individually.

from lower left to upper right, is always visible in the southern sky during winter (only) from anywhere in North America, as is the Big Dipper, whose tail is close enough to north to be used as a reference.

Index

About the Author

Len McDougall is the author of the following books: *The Encyclopedia of Tracks & Scats*; *The Log Cabin: An Adventure in Self Reliance, Individualism, and Cabin Building*; *The Field & Stream Wilderness Survival Handbook*; *The Complete Tracker*; *Practical Outdoor Projects*; *Practical Outdoor Survival*; *The Snowshoe Handbook*; *The Outdoors Almanac,* and *Made for the Outdoors.*

He is also a wilderness guide and survival instructor for Timberwolf Wilderness Adventures, Paradise, Michigan.